THE JUST SHALL LIVE BY FAITH

BLESSED ARE THEY
THAT
HAVE NOT SEEN,
YET
HAVE
BELIEVED

by
T.K. Williams

Vision Publishing
Montgomery, Alabama

Scripture quotations are taken from one of the
following translations of the Bible:

The Holy Bible King James Version, Ed. 3,
The Holy Bible New King James Version, Ed. 3
The Message: The Bible in Contemporary Language, Ed. 3
New Testament in Modern Speech, Ed. 1
Young's Literal Translation of the Bible, Ed. 1
The Holy Bible American Standard Version, Ed. 1
God's Word, Ed. 1
The Holman Christian Standard Bible

Copyright (c) 2009 FindEx.com, Inc., and its licensors
Used by permission of QuickVerse

Published by:
Vision Publishing
P.O. Box 242031
Montgomery, AL 36124

Copyright © 2009 by T.K. Williams.

ISBN 978-0-578-05053-9

Contributing Editor: Yolanda Huntley

The Just Shall Live by Faith:
Blessed Are they that
Have Not Seen, Yet Have Believed (John 20:29)

Printed and bound in the United States of America. All rights reserved. Except for brief excerpts used in reviews, no portion of this work may be reproduced or published without expressed written permission from the author or the author's agent.

Second Edition

DEDICATION

This book is dedicated first to
my Heavenly Father who is my Creator,
To Jesus Christ who is my Lord and Shepherd,
To the Holy Spirit who is my Helper, and Teacher, and then to:
Max, Courtney & Kaela who love and support me,
To my parents Mr. William and Cynthia Ruth
who gave me life,
My Aunt and Uncle, Roy and Gwendolyn Thomas
To my brothers and sisters who are always there for me
To Pastors Steven and Yolanda Huntley,
To Pastors Anthony and Kelly McMillan,
To Pastor Rander Draper
to my church family at True Divine Baptist Church and all who have all helped to lay my spiritual foundation.

To every friend that God has given me and cheered me on even when I wanted to quit,
and most of all this is written in loving memory of
Mary Lena Bell, my
grandmother who helped to build my spiritual foundation.

Thank you for what you have been to me in my life, and helping me to
become all that the Father has ordained.

PRAYER OF SALVATION

If you are looking for completeness, look no further. Say this prayer if you would like to know the One, and true, Savior, and King. If you are looking for completion in your life, continue reading.

Jesus Christ can help you put the broken pieces back together in your life. Your first step is to ask Him to come into your life and reign as Lord and King.

If you would like to invite Christ into your life, take a moment right now, and make this prayer personal between you and God. Watch for the first time how His presence will come alive in your life.

Dear Lord, I come to you right now with every part of my being. I am searching for something that I now realize only you can give me. I have come to know that in order to be a part of your Kingdom I must confess according to Romans 10:9-10. So right now, I confess with my mouth and say "Jesus Christ, I want you to be Lord of my life. I believe in my heart that you died on the cross for my sins. I also believe in my heart that God raised you from the dead and you are now seated on the right hand of His throne. So now Lord, I confess that I have sinned against you, but through your love for me, you have made the Blood of Jesus a covering for my sins. Because of His sacrifice and love for me, I now live according to the righteousness of Jesus Christ. Lord, I also know that according to your Word, that there is a baptism of the Holy Spirit and fire. I ask you right now, to baptize me with your Holy Spirit, and I receive this Baptism by faith. Thank you Father, Son, and the Holy Spirt, for your love towards me. My life is now in your hands. In Jesus Christ name I pray" Amen.

If you have prayed this prayer, and believe your confession, we welcome you into the Kingdom of God. Angels are now rejoicing over you! Make a commitment this day to find a church home that teaches you the Word of God. You will begin to gain knowledge about your Heavenly Father, His Son, and His Holy Spirit.

CONTENTS

CHAPTER 1. WHAT IS FAITH?..13

CHAPTER 2. FAITH MUST BE DEMONSTRATED.............25

CHAPTER 3. YOUR FAITH AND YOUR HEALING.........45

CHAPTER 4. FAITH AND YOUR FINANCES.......................55

CHAPTER 5. FAITH AND YOUR RELATIONSHIPS.........63

CHAPTER 6. FAITH AND ETERNITY..71

CHAPTER 7. FAITH AND THE FIGHT......................................79

CHAPTER 8. FAITH AND HIS RIGHTEOUSNESS.............85

CHAPTER 9. FAITH AND HIS LOVE..97

CHAPTER 10. FAITH IN JESUS CHRIST...............................105

CHAPTER 11. FAITH IN HIS HOLY SPIRIT...........................111

CHAPTER 12. FAITH IN THE FATHER...................................117

CHAPTER 13. FAITH IN HIS RESURRECTION...................127

CHAPTER 14. FAITH…OUR ONLY OPTION.......................137

INTRODUCTION

This book is written from a direct instruction from God. He has given me the words of this book that I now share with you. This book addresses His people about the subject of faith so that we may learn how to apply our faith, and face life situations and circumstances with a Holy confidence in God. The words of this book speak about the importance of faith and how His children are instructed to believe in Him, and His Word. The title, **The Just Shall Live by Faith**, is based on the scripture from Habakkuk 2:4.

>*...but the just shall live by his faith*

In the times we live in, it is imperative that God's children understand what it means to live by faith. Besides love, faith is the foundation on which we live our lives, and is required of every believer. It is my desire that after you have finished reading this book, you will see God's power in your life, and that your only option is to live by faith. God is able, you just have to believe…

It is my hope that you use this book along with your bible to manifest the following verse in your life:

>*"But ye beloved, building up yourselves on your most holy faith,…" (Jude 1:20).*

Chapter 1

WHAT IS FAITH?

What is faith? What is the purpose of faith? How do we demonstrate faith? What are we supposed to have faith in? Faith in whom? How do we live by faith?

These questions and many more will be answered. By the assistance of the Holy Spirit, our teacher and guide, we shall learn and begin to experience life at a new level. We will understand what it means to live by faith like never before.

As we live this life, where is our focus? Can we truly see what we need to see? Are we able to experience the Spirit realm in which the Lord moves, or do we only experience what we see by our natural physical eye? Which eye do you live by? Do you live by your natural or spiritual eye? As believers, how do we begin to shift our perspective to see how God sees? How can we see through the eyes of faith?

Now let's consider faith. Faith is immeasurable. Faith may constantly increase or decrease. Faith is more valuable than anything we have access to. Faith is the core, and the very foundation of our belief system. If you are saved, faith is what keeps you saved. It is the foundation on which we experience God and His kingdom. The question is are you experiencing the Kingdom of God, or do you merely know about the Kingdom of God?

In the times we live in, we hear various amounts of teaching on how to express and demonstrate our faith. The question comes to mind, "What is the Lord saying about our walk of faith?" Why is it that some have the evidence of faith, and some do not?

We must start with faith in God's Word. Whatever that Word is, it is our responsibility to believe it. It may be His written Word, or His spoken Word – the key is faith in His Word, not our words, and not our beliefs.

The first step in living by faith is to respond to His Word. In order to become a disciple of Christ, it was necessary that we responded to His Word by making a confession with our mouths, and believing in our hearts (Romans 10:9-10). We

What is Faith?

must develop the skill of distinguishing our words from His Words or the world's words. We must ask ourselves, "What is the Lord saying?" This is the first step in living by faith. It is to know that God's Words will never fail. That He alone is faithful to fulfill his good promises. His Word states, "Not by power, not by might, but by my Spirit," says the Lord (Zechariah 4:6).

It is not by our own individual power that we may live, but it is faith in our Heavenly Father. Faith in action is an act of obedience, or a response to what the Lord is saying to us. According to His Word, "Faith is the substance of things hoped for, the evidence of things not seen" (Hebrews 11:1). Hope and trust, builds faith. Placing trust in the Lord, hoping in His Word, relying on His promises, are the foundations of faith.

Trusting in the Lord is a necessity. In our society, as in all others, living by faith is a necessity. In the times we live in, we have used our faith to gain better jobs, faith to build and purchase houses, faith to gain money, promotions…the list goes on and on. There is nothing wrong in desiring these things. It only becomes an issue, once our faith is used only on self-centered wants and needs for our personal benefit. In James chapter 4 verse 3 it states:

"You ask and don't receive because you ask with wrong motives, so that you may spend it on your evil desires." Yes, we do have needs, and the Lord knows that. Yes, we are to use our faith in our everyday lives; but what about using our faith to advance the Kingdom of God? Do we use our faith to promote the Kingdom of God? Do you have enough faith to use it to heal others? Does your faith set captives free? Does your faith heal the broken-hearted? Does your faith proclaim liberty for those that are bound? This is promoting the Kingdom of God.

It is a testimony to our true affection and desires when a car, job, promotion, or a house is the only evidence of our faith level. The Lord says "Where your treasure is, your heart will be there" (Matthew 6:21).

So what is faith? "Now faith is the substance of things hoped for, the evidence of things not seen." (Hebrews 11:1) We must believe first, and then we will see. Jesus said to Thomas, "Blessed is the man who believes before He sees" (John 20:29).

We live in a world in which the opposite appears to be true. We let circumstances dictate our decisions. We run our homes and businesses on what we see in the natural. We forget that we are a joint-heir with Christ (Romans 8:17). When you study the instance in which Jesus fed over five thousand with two fish and five loaves of bread, it is challenging for the human mind to conceive how this could be accomplished. Jesus began with a small amount (what appeared to be not enough), yet ended with more than enough. The disciples could not see beyond their natural eye, and based their decisions merely on what they could see. But Jesus knew. Jesus saw beyond the natural.

What is Faith?

He accessed a realm by His faith in who He was, and faith in who God was. How could two fish and five loaves of bread feed 5000 people? There isn't one math course that will teach that. But in the spiritual realm, faith calls things that be not, as if they were (Romans 4:17). For example, in the beginning, light was created because God called it. The sky became the sky because God called it. The fish and the fowl of the air were created because God called it (Genesis 1). What are you calling? Do you have evidence of your spoken faith?

Where can we find *spoken faith* in God's Word? God gave us a great model in the beginning- in Genesis. But we tend to overlook His creative power. We tend to say, "Yeah, but that was God. What does that have to do with me?" Remember in His Word He said, "You will do much greater works than this" (John 14:12). The Father designed a system that is meant to be utilized by believers. We have at times, a "form of godliness, denying the power…" (2 Timothy 3:5). What good is our knowledge of the scriptures, without use and application? It is similar to knowing mathematics, but never knowing when to actually add, subtract, or multiply. Let's take a moment and look at faith in action. Take a minute and read the account of Peter, when he attempted to walk on water found in Matthew chapter 14.

First of all, remember that Peter was in the right place at the right time to utilize his faith. He was with the Master. Remember, faith comes from the Master. Nevertheless, look at the scene. Peter is in the boat with the other disciples.

Peter is the one who recognized Jesus walking on the water. Peter seized the opportunity to use his faith. He could have remained like the other disciples, yet he decided to use his faith. He said to Jesus, "Master, if it is you, bid me to come to you on the water". (Matthew 14:28) Peter recognized that he carried a power within him that would defy natural conditions. This is what we could call "water-walking faith". Within the logical realm, it appears that water could not sustain Peter's weight, "but with God, all things are possible, to them that believe" (Matthew 19:26). It wasn't until Peter began to observe his natural conditions that his faith began to waiver. From this account we can see that Peter clearly began with success. As long as his faith opposed natural conditions, he could walk on the water. But the moment natural conditions conquered his faith, he began to sink. In verse 31 Jesus replied, "Why did you doubt? "

Doubt is a strong influence in the mind. But faith in action may conquer doubt. Doubt tells us to observe natural conditions, whereas faith tells us to consider supernatural conditions. We cannot look at natural conditions as the final answer. Let's face it; it is not easy to have "water-walking" faith, most of us our stumbling on dry ground, let alone water. We may not attempt to walk on water, but some of the circumstances we face in our lives will require that our level of faith increase. However, no matter the circumstances, faith may be required. For instance, if you are facing financial difficulties, you may need to have faith that God will provide an increase as you remain faithful in tithing. This may require "water-walking" faith. Our health issues at times will require "water-walking" faith. Mending broken relationships may require "water-walking" faith. Regardless of the circumstances, your faith tells you to believe God.

When we are trying to achieve our goals, aspirations and dreams, it may require" water-walking" faith. So, why is it so difficult? Why are we challenged to believe the impossible? It should be obvious to us.

Despite our challenges, demonstrated faith in the life of a believer glorifies God. Jesus himself said, "How can you not believe me, when you see the works that I do?" (John 10:25) Remember Lazarus? Jesus said, "Thy brother will rise again" (John 11:23). In essence, Jesus said this situation only exist, so that you can see the glory of my Father (John 11:40). It is not that Jesus Christ merely spoke about the Kingdom of God, but that He demonstrated the Kingdom of God. The same requirement exists for believers today. God's Word states, "Faith without works is dead" (James 2:26). Faith and works go "hand in hand". It is time for the family of God to demonstrate their faith and give glory to God. We must call forth finances, call forth healing, call forth mended relationships, and call forth the provisions of the Kingdom of God. It is by our works through Christ that we demonstrate our faith. Remember, "For with God nothing shall be impossible" (Luke 1:37). **Believing in God** is the foundation, but **believing God** is the work (John 6:29). To demonstrate the Kingdom, we must go to work.

What can we say then? Will we fail to display the Kingdom of God because of our unbelief? Faith is believing God. Faith says God can be trusted. Faith demonstrates His Kingdom, and accesses the lifestyle that He has supremely designed for us.

So the question from this account becomes, what can I learn from this instance? How can I defy my natural conditions and move to the place God is calling me to? Do I have enough faith to cause me to move beyond my circumstances? Remember, ***the just shall live by faith***. So, what can we say about faith? "Now faith is the substance of things hoped for and the evidence of things not seen" (Hebrews 11:1).

So, what evidence are you looking at? If we base our lives and decisions on what is seen, we are not living by faith. To live by faith, is to live in another dimension spiritually, while we live in what merely seems like a physical world. Having faith is when we base our decisions and life choices on God's promises and His Word. It is to trust in God who lives in an unseen realm, not available to the natural eye. This kind of faith requires spiritual focus. This kind of faith requires us to live life with the expectation that "all is well" (2 Kings 4:8-27). It is the kind of faith that will sometimes require an immediate response. Remember Peter?

In the scriptures, does it say that Peter sat and pondered or thought about getting out of the boat? No. Peter put his faith into action immediately. A faith response is a direct reflection of what you are hoping for. It is time to take an evaluation.

What is Faith?

What are you hoping for? Is your hope aligned with the will of the Father? To have hope is to have everything. Long ago, one of the most famous quotes in the culture of African-Americans was "Keep hope alive!" (Jesse Jackson, July 19, 1988, Democratic National Convention Address)

This was not just a faddish quote, but a prescription for life. It is imperative that we keep hoping. It is important that we keep our hope alive by taking opportunities to use our faith. As a true disciple of Christ, "keeping hope alive" requires us to demonstrate our faith.

So when we take a moment and think, how do we demonstrate our faith? Can you see faith working daily in your life? Why is it so important? Isn't it enough to have faith? Before answering those questions, take a moment and look at the scripture below,

James 2:18-26 (ASV) 18Yea, a man will say, Thou hast faith, and I have works: show me thy faith apart from thy works, and I by my works will show thee my faith. 19Thou believest that God is one; thou doest well: the demons also believe, and shudder. 20But wilt thou know, O vain man, that faith apart from works is barren? 21Was not Abraham our father justified by works, in that he offered up Isaac his son upon the altar? 22Thou seest that faith wrought with his works, and by works was faith made perfect; 23and the scripture was fulfilled which saith, And Abraham believed God, and it was reckoned unto him for righteousness; and he was called the friend of God. 24Ye see that by works a man is justified, and not only by faith. 25And in like manner was not also Rahab the harlot justified by works, in that she received the messengers, and sent them out another way? 26For as the body apart from the spirit is dead, even so faith apart from works is dead.

If no other scripture convinces us, this scripture surely does. According to James, if we do not have works to accompany our faith, we ascribe no higher than demons. It is imperative that with our faith, we have corresponding action. James tells us that our faith is demonstrated by our works. So the question becomes, what qualifies as works? This is the area, in which we have great flexibility.

Works may be needed for personal situations and circumstances such as healing, finances, jobs, and relationships. Our works display the glory of God. For instance, working as a missionary, or letting God give you a healing ministry are examples of faith in action. No matter what the works are, we have a great teacher who has led by example - Jesus Christ. Whenever we need to understand any biblical concept, we must look to Jesus. What were His works on earth?

Remember Lazarus: When Jesus heard that, he said, This sickness is not unto death, but for the glory of God, that the Son of God might be glorified thereby (John 11:4) Take a look. The Lord's works ranged from healing blind men, men with leprosy, casting out demons, feeding the poor, preaching the gospel, and much more. Notice, that Jesus' works were "other-centered". He stated that:

Mark 10:43-45 (ASV) 43But it is not so among you: but whosoever would become great among you, shall be your minister; 44and whosoever would be first among you, shall be servant of all. 45For the Son of man also came not to be ministered unto, but to minister, and to give his life a ransom for many.

So although we are to demonstrate our faith, our faith should be used also to benefit others. To truly be first in Kingdom of God, we must first put others before ourselves. So the point is that faith is not a tool given by God to be abused, but a tool that helps to establish his Kingdom. It is not a tool used to merely gain houses, jobs, and possessions, but a gift from God to be used to demonstrate His power and glory. So, faith is a big deal. Faith is the manner which we access our miracles.

There are several miracles in God's Word in which Jesus asked the person, "Do you believe?" It is as though, before He would demonstrate His works, Jesus would check to see if the person would believe before the miracle was manifested. So if you are prone to believe "that faith stuff doesn't work," there isn't a problem with faith, the problem may be with your level of faith. Remember, "According to your faith, be it unto you" (Matthew 9:29). He is asking us today, "Do you believe?" If so, be it unto you according to your faith.

Chapter 2

FAITH MUST BE DEMONSTRATED

Now take a moment and think, when did you last demonstrate your faith? Ok, when was the last time you demonstrated your faith on behalf of someone else? We are all in this together; demonstrating faith is not an easy task, because it causes you to place all fears and possibilities of failure aside. Quite honestly, it seems easier to never believe anything, and not risk failure, than it is to believe, and risk making mistakes. But the honest truth is that if our hearts are right before God, He will cover our mistakes. Using a basketball analogy, consider this quote concerning mistakes

"You will always miss 100% of the shots you don't take".

Living in the kingdom requires that you take a few shots. Some shots may make it in, others may not, but at least you are in the game. One of the best scriptures in the bible is a reference to Samuel the prophet. It is stated in I Samuel:

1 Samuel 3:19-21 (ASV) 19And Samuel grew, and Jehovah was with him, and did let none of his words fall to the ground. 20And all Israel from Dan even to Beer-sheba knew that Samuel was established to be a prophet of Jehovah. 21And Jehovah appeared again in Shiloh; for Jehovah revealed himself to Samuel in Shiloh by the word of Jehovah.

What a great testimony of what it means to dwell with God and live by His Word. It says that none of Samuel's words fell to the ground. This requires faith in God. To know that when you speak or act on behalf of God's Kingdom, that He is with you, and will establish you and your words. That is what you would call making 100% of the shots.

Take a look another passage of scripture:

1 Corinthians 2:1-5 (ASV) 1And I, brethren, when I came unto you, came not with excellency of speech or of wisdom, proclaiming to you the testimony of God. 2For I determined not to know anything among you, save Jesus Christ, and him crucified. 3And I was with you in weakness, and in fear, and in much trembling. 4And my speech and my preaching were not in persuasive words of wisdom, but in demonstration of the Spirit and of power: 5that your faith should not stand in the wisdom of men, but in the power of God.

Notice the Apostle Paul's words, "demonstration of the Spirit and of power". Paul emphasized that his ministry could not be validated on the basis of faith or words alone, but in the demonstration of power. Jesus Christ also made this point when he stated, "you shall know the tree by the fruit it bears" (Matthew 7:15-20). To be an effective member in the Kingdom of God, it is not merely our faith that validates us, but our fruit that is produced by our faith.

It may be established, that faith and works go hand in hand. The question becomes, not only will you use your faith, but how will you use your faith? Will your works testify for you when you enter the Lord's presence? This is what we are striving for to "store up treasures in heaven, not here on earth where moths and rust destroy" (Matthew 6:19). Faith helps you to store your treasures in heaven.

Now let's take a moment and consider what Jesus said,

Luke 18:8 (MSNT) 8Yes, He will soon avenge their wrongs. Yet, when the Son of Man comes, will He find faith on earth?"

This statement comes from Jesus, and He is demonstrating to His disciples the need for diligence and persistence in prayer.

To be a part of the Kingdom of God, it is imperative that believers have "persistent faith".

A good example is found in chapter 18 of Luke. Here we can find a widow woman who demonstrates "persistent faith". If you read the account in Luke 18 you see that the widow is persistent in pursuing justice from the unrighteous judge. Now remember, the Lord is righteous. If the widow was able to receive her answer from an unrighteous judge, how much more can we expect from a righteous King? Jesus is asking us, when He returns, when He comes in His glory, will He find faith in you? Will he find you living by faith? Will he find you persistent in prayer? Will he find you demanding justice for the Kingdom of God?

Jesus Christ is demonstrating our need to be strong in our faith. He is looking for our faith. ***It's impossible to please God apart from faith. And why? Because anyone who wants to approach God must believe both that he exists and that he cares enough to respond to those who seek him*** (Hebrews 11:6, Message).

Hopefully you are convinced of the need for demonstrated faith in your life. But the importance of faith is its use and practical applications. In the times we are living in with dis- ease on the rise, poverty knocking at the doors, crime at an all-time high, children on drugs, homosexuality on the rise, what other choice do we have? How can we apply our faith?

Learning to apply our faith requires that we learn from Jesus. What else did Jesus do during His ministry on earth? If you think back to Mary, the mother of Jesus, one of the most important conversations found in the bible, was between herself and the angel Gabriel:

Luke 1:37-38 (ASV) 37For no word from God shall be void of power. 38And Mary said, Behold, the handmaid of the Lord; be it unto me according to thy word. And the angel departed from her.

Mary knew the importance in believing a Word from the Lord. In order for the Savior to be born through the Virgin Mary, it required faith on Mary's behalf. She responded, "Be it unto me according to thy word." Now look back at Jesus' statement "according to thy faith, be it unto you". Do you see the similarity? Most of all do not forget the statement from Gabriel, "for no word from God shall be void of power".

Without the faith of Mary, she would not have become the Mother of Christ. She had faith in God's Word. Mary does not operate in doubt and unbelief. She immediately accepts God's Word, and knows that "he is able to do this". This record of history demonstrates to us that faith is not an option, but a requirement if we are to receive all that God has preplanned and designed for us. Do you desire children? "According to your faith, be it unto you." Do you desire to start your own business? "According to your faith, be it unto you." Do you dream of being debt free? "According to your faith be it unto you". Remember, all things are possible to those that believe.

Mark 9:23 (ASV) 23And Jesus said unto him, If thou canst! All things are possible to him that believeth.

Believe what? Believe that "no word from God shall be void of power". That is the key - we are not required to have faith in our plans, or our desires, but those desires and plans must be birthed from a Word from God. Without a Word, you don't need a business. Without a Word, you don't need a new job. Without a Word, you don't need to move to a new city. The key is faith in His Word, not our words.

Too many of us are disappointed because we are waiting on manifestations of things God has not given a Word for. Mary had faith in His Word, and in His timing. She did not set out on her own to have the son she desired, in the way she desired. Think about that; surely Mary would have desired to birth Jesus in the traditional manner, and avoid the persecution and disappointment that sometimes comes with obeying God. Jesus was not birthed from Mary's desire, but from God's. Do you remember the portion of the Lord's Prayer that states, "thy kingdom come, thy will be done"? Is your faith and what you believe God for based on His will or your will? Jesus stated these words in the Garden of Gethsemane- "Nevertheless, not my will, but thy will be done" (Matthew 26:39). Do you have a "nevertheless" in your spirit? We will try to understand what it really means to believe. Take a look at the definition.

The Greek word for believe is *pisteuo* which means:

1) to think to be true, to be persuaded of, to credit, place confidence in
2) to credit, have confidence, in a moral or religious reference
3) used in the NT of the conviction and trust to which a man is impelled by a certain inner and higher prerogative and law of soul
4) to trust in Jesus or God as able to aid either in obtaining or in doing something: saving faith
5) mere acknowledgment of some fact or event: intellectual faith
6) to entrust a thing to one, i.e. his fidelity

(Blue Letter Bible. "Dictionary and Word Search for pisteuō (Strong's 4100)". Blue Letter Bible. 1996-2009. 26 Jan 2009)

Now let's focus on a few words in this definition-persuaded, place confidence in, conviction, trust, acknowledgement or to entrust. When we believe God we are persuaded, confident, convicted and trusting, that what He says will come to pass-that what He has carefully designed for our lives is what is best. He is waiting to move on our behalf, but it requires that we trust Him with all of our heart (Proverbs 3:5-6).

Well, let's not be naïve. It is difficult to trust when bills are piling high, our health may be declining, or children just will not "act right". If you carefully study the great men and women in the Bible, you will clearly see that there were times when their faith was challenged. Take a moment; think about Daniel in the lion's den, and Shadrach, Meshach, and Abednego placed in the fiery furnace. Don't stop there. What about Paul and Silas? Moses? Esther? All throughout the Bible we see that it required great faith to stand in the midst of trials. So then, what is our excuse? Why does our faith fail so quickly and easily? The Lord declared:

Matthew 24:4-14 (MSNT) 4"Take care that no one misleads you," answered Jesus; 5"for many will come assuming my name and saying 'I am the Christ;' and they will mislead many. 6And before long you will hear of wars and rumors of wars. Do not be alarmed, for such things must be; but the End is not yet. 7For nation will rise in arms against nation, kingdom against kingdom, and there will be famines and earthquakes in various places; 8but all these miseries are but like the early pains of childbirth. 9"At that time they will deliver you up to punishment and will put you to death; and you will be objects of hatred to all the nations because you are called by my name. 10Then will many stumble and fall, and they will betray one another and hate one another. 11Many false prophets will rise up and lead multitudes astray; 12and because of the prevalent disregard of God's law the love of the great majority will grow cold; 13but those who stand firm to the End shall be saved. 14And this Good News of the Kingdom shall be proclaimed throughout the whole world to set the evidence before all the Gentiles; and then the End will come.

These events are taking place now. Nations are against nation. The love of the majority has grown cold and earthquakes are in various places. As people of God, we are called to discern the times. Living by faith requires that we stand in the midst of turmoil and despair. With an economy in upheaval, spirits of depression and oppression on the rise, do we have a choice? What is the alternative? Do we walk with our heads hung down, confessing what we see, instead of what we are hoping for? Take a moment and look at the last part, "the Good news of the Kingdom". As saints of God, we are still hoping for the Good news. We are to proclaim the "Good News". But first we are called to believe in the "Good News".

How can we proclaim to another, something that we ourselves fail to believe in? There is good news knowing that we are a part of the Kingdom-that we reign in life through Christ Jesus (Romans 5:17). We serve a great High Priest, and His name is Jesus Christ.

We are to live by every Word that He has spoken and declared, and to live by that Word, requires belief not only in Him, but also in what He says. Jesus Christ is the author and finisher of our faith (Hebrews 12:2).

Remember, faith is "the substance of things hoped for, the evidence of things not seen" (Hebrews 11:1). The Kingdom of God is not based on what you see (Luke 17:21). Kingdom benefits can only be accessed by your faith, and then seen. What are those benefits? Kingdom benefits include healing, restoration, renewal, salvation, prosperity, protection, and much more. Our faith serves as a lifeline that connects us to our benefits. It is important to remember that with God, all things are possible (Matthew 19:26). Usually, if we are not receiving our Kingdom benefits, please know, there is nothing wrong with God, the problem may lie within our ability to believe God.

Walking by faith may not be an easy task, but we have examples of men and women of God who have demonstrated to us how to live by faith. Let us take a moment and focus on one of the widows in the Bible. This event is recorded in the book of II Kings chapter 4.

2 Kings 4:1-7 (ASV) 1Now there cried a certain woman of the wives of the sons of the prophets unto Elisha, saying, Thy servant my husband is dead; and thou knowest that thy servant did fear Jehovah: and the creditor is come to take unto him my two children to be bondmen. 2And Elisha said unto her, what shall I do for thee? tell me; what hast thou in the house? And she said, Thy handmaid hath not anything in the house, save a pot of oil. 3Then he said, Go, borrow thee vessels abroad of all thy neighbors, even empty vessels; borrow not a few. 4And thou shalt go in, and shut the door upon thee and upon thy sons, and pour out into all those vessels; and thou shalt set aside that which is full. 5So she went from him, and shut the door upon her and upon her sons; they brought the vessels to her, and she poured out. 6And it came to pass, when the vessels were full, that she said unto her son, Bring me yet a vessel. And he said unto her, there is not a vessel more. And the oil stayed. 7Then she came and told the man of God. And he said, Go, sell the oil, and pay thy debt, and live thou and thy sons of the rest.

As you read this passage take a moment and focus on one fact. Notice; the oil did not stop until the vessels ran out. Think about this. What if her sons brought the vessels from not only their neighbors, but from everyone in their neighborhood? Elisha told the widow "borrow not a few". He never indicated or defined what "a few" represented. The number was determined by the faith of her sons. The sons brought her the number of vessels that they expected they would fill. Their faith, determined their oil. Notice, the widow expected more vessels because she said, "Bring me yet a vessel". This statement indicates that the widow thought that her sons had more vessels.

This scripture demonstrates what is happening today. God is still pouring the oil. He pours the oil in our relationships. He pours the oil in our ministries. He pours the oil in our finances. He pours the oil on our health. But how much of the oil you receive, depends solely on the number of vessels you provide. In other words, how much faith do you contain? If you were in the same situation as the widow, how many vessels would you have provided? Remember God said,

Malachi 3:1 (ASV) 1Behold, I send my messenger, and he shall prepare the way before me: and the Lord, whom ye seek, will suddenly come to his temple; and the messen- ger of the covenant, whom ye desire, behold, he cometh, saith Jehovah of hosts. I will pour you out a blessing that you do not have room enough to receive.

God is pouring. How much of His oil can you contain? Are His blessings overflowing in your life? He said you don't have enough room to receive it. In other words, you could not begin to collect enough vessels to contain God's oil. Your faith should have no limitations. Your faith should cause you to "borrow not a few" and stand and receive the overflowing blessings of God.

Ok, now it should be established. Faith is important. So as believers, we must understand how to increase our faith. When you take a look at the scriptures, it states that faith comes by hearing and hearing by the Word of God (Romans 10:17). Before we can live by faith, we have to understand how God increases our faith. God's Word helps to establish our faith. It says in the book of 2 Chronicles 20:20, "Believe God, and so shall you be established, believe His prophets and you will prosper." Having faith requires believing God. Believing God comes from hearing and knowing the Word.

Since faith comes by hearing, then we must position ourselves to hear.

Hearing comes in many forms; attending and becoming part of a congregation that focuses on teaching you God's Word, focusing your time on studying God's Word, listening to praise and worship music, listening throughout the week to strong ministries provided on the Internet, TV, or radio.

In our country we are surrounded with the opportunity to hear God's Word. With technological advancements, hearing the Word is as easy as breathing. Just do it! But remember, the level to which we hear depends on our priorities. In life it is easy to become distracted with the routine of life. Picking up children, cooking dinner, attending to our mates, working, and many other factors crowd our lives and sometimes hinder us from positioning ourselves to clearly hear God's Word.

There are two main ways in which we can hear God and build our faith. One method comes from the logos. This is God's written Word. This is when we hear God, and learn about His kingdom from the written Word.

The bible says that "they gave themselves over to studying the scriptures, to see if what they were stating was true" (Acts17:11). We are called to give ourselves over to studying the scriptures. Not only to make sure that His messengers are true messengers, but to hear God's truths. The other method is what is called *rhema*. This is where God reveals himself or speaks a particular message to us. It is usually referred to as a revelation. For instance, you may be studying the scriptures, and find that a particular verse catches your attention. This is God's Spirit magnifying a particular scripture. This is God's way of communicating with us while we are studying. Remember, "God's Word is alive, powerful, and sharper than a double edge sword" (Hebrews 4:12).

The scripture that is speaking to you comes alive in your heart. After you give your attention to that scripture, it is important for you to guard the Word God is trying to implant in your heart. Remember, Satan attempts to steal the Word out of your heart-especially a rhema Word (Luke 8:12).

You may also experience His *rhema* Word in various ways. Once we begin to discipline ourselves and learn how to wait on hearing God, you will begin to hear that "still small voice" (I Kings 19:12). For instance, when you begin to build your "most holy faith" (Jude 1:20), built on the Word of God, you will begin to hear God communicate in another way. For example, you might find yourself in prayer, or simply going through your day, then all of a sudden you hear a quiet voice say, "The things that are impossible with men, are possible with God" (Luke 18:27). At first, you may feel as though you need to be "checked in". You may feel not only crazy- but the certified, documented, clinical condition of crazy. After experiences like this begin to increase, you will begin to realize that it is the very voice of God. The question is why

Faith Must Be Demonstrated

would we not believe? Throughout the Bible, we read of men and women whom God spoke to. Do we believe that God has stopped speaking? Or better yet, maybe we have stopped hearing. We have to position ourselves to hear; sifting through the noise in the world. You know, the noise that says, "you can't make it', or "just give up, it is no use anyways". This noise works in opposition to our faith. It is designed to crush our faith. This voice is satanic, and meant to destroy your faith in God. So in today's culture and climate, we do not have a choice, we must hear. We must discern His voice. God's Word states: "My sheep respond to my voice, and I know who they are. They follow me" (God's Word Translation). Remember, it is not easy, but it is possible. It is a matter of positioning ourselves.

Understanding the importance of hearing is critical, yet even more critical is what we do after we have heard. His word says, "Be ye doers of the Word not hearers only" (James 1:22). That is the crisis. Many of us in the church today are suffering from "hearingitis". What is that? Hearing, and never accomplishing and activating the Word we hear. The Bible says that this man is like a man who sees his image in the mirror, and walks away immediately forgetting his own image (James 1:23). That's powerful! This could also mean that it is difficult to see who we really are without God's Word. It is as though His Word holds our unique image. But it is important that we apply the Word we hear, to avoid forgetting who we are in God. Think about it. Even Eve suffered from "hearingitis". She received a direct rhema Word from God. But that Word was not sown in her heart. Satan, was right there waiting to steal the Word from her heart. Sometimes applying the Word, just means that we hold onto it with everything in us. Eve was a woman who forgot her image. God had already provided everything she needed. He had carefully designated all that belonged to her and Adam. God gave one stipulation – don't touch this particular tree. Sometimes the Word from God is an instruction given to us to protect us. God said that he would be her provider, protector, advisor and friend. Remember the scripture, "Believe God and so shall ye be established?" (2 Chronicles 2:20). Adam and Eve failed to do this. They received the rhema, but failed to be a doer with the Word God had given them.

Many of us complain about Adam and Eve, but if we were to take a true examination of our level of faith, would we pass the test? Adam and Eve had one challenge-to believe God. Throughout the bible you will see that this test has not changed- Noah, Abraham, Sarah, Moses, Isaac, Joseph, David, Shadrach, Meshach, Abednego, Jonah, Gideon, Rahab, Deborah, Esther, and many more. These are among the heroes of faith (Hebrews 11). You see, "this is the victory that overcomes the world – our faith" (1 John 5:4). These men and women of God could not overcome their circumstances without their faith. We have more written scriptures than they did at the time, so what is our excuse? If we think that God is going to write a new command that states, "Thou shalt not believe" we are fooling ourselves. We have TV, radio, Internet, mega-churches, iPod bibles, mp3 bibles, New

Faith Must Be Demonstrated

Living Translations, the Message translation, NIV… and the list goes on and on, but the minute we lose our jobs, we are powerless, ineffective, doubtful and anxious. So what is the problem? Accessibility to His Word is not an obstacle. So how can we increase our faith?

This answer is found in one scripture; "Lord, help my unbelief" (Mark 9:24). It is time to be honest with God. We must let Him know, "God I am struggling, I don't know if I have enough faith for this. Can you help me? Can you help my unbelief?" (Mark 9:24) God will do it. He says that he hears the prayers of the righteous and that "His strength is made perfect in our weakness" (2 Corinthians 12:9). Unbelief and doubt are weaknesses, but He is the Sovereign God, who can help our unbelief. It only takes time, trust and experiences. Experiences with God build faith, and faith builds trust in God.

Experiences are key. Even with a great man of God like Moses, you will see that he not only heard from God, but he experienced God. When Moses spoke with God, he saw a bush burning, yet the bush was not consumed. The bush is what attracted Moses' attention (Exodus 3). But wait, let's not stop there. What about the parting of the Red Sea, the manna and the quail pouring down from heaven, and the ten plagues sent to Egypt? The list goes on and on. If you aren't convinced, think about Abraham. The birth of his son Isaac, the ram in the bush, the increase in cattle, silver and gold, what about the rescue of Lot? Living without the experiences of God is like baking a cake without yeast, attempting to send an email without an Internet connection, sleeping on a pillowcase without a pillow. Experiencing God, demonstrates who He is. It shows us that He is Jehovah Shammah- the God who is there, or Jehovah Roi – the God who sees you. Through personal experiences He is saying, "See! I told you I am here, remember "I am that, I am." (Exodus 3:14) Through personal experiences He is saying, I am your provider, I am your way-maker, I am your divine initiator, I am the light on your pathway, I am your warrior, I am your restorer, I will show you that I am whatever your faith allows Me to be. Start today looking for your personal experiences with God, accessing those experiences by faith. Call forth those things you need, and watch God demonstrate His awesome power and greatness.

Psalms 145 says, "God is great and worthy to be praised- His greatness in unsearchable." Your mind cannot even conceive the greatness of Yaweh. He can be your strong tower, shield, strength, friend, company keeper or way-maker. He desires to reveal himself to you as your Lord and Savior Has God revealed Himself to you? We all have situations and circumstances in our lives, which will throw us curve balls. We sometimes find ourselves wandering "can I see my way through?" Just know this is the opportune time in which God desires to show himself strong in our lives if we will allow Him.

Faith Must Be Demonstrated

Chapter 3

YOUR FAITH AND YOUR HEALING

One of the most important facts about Jesus Christ is that Jesus is a healer. Several instances within the Bible demonstrate the power of Jesus Christ and His desire to heal all. Consider this scripture:

They came, tons of them, bringing along the paraplegic, the blind, the maimed, the mute - all sorts of people in need - and more or less threw them down at Jesus' feet to see what he would do with them. He healed them. (Matthew 15:30 – Message)

So, the question is what does that have to do with us? Sure we all believe Jesus could heal because He is the Messiah, the

Savior, and the Holy One of Israel. Well, the fact of the matter is that it has a lot to do with us. Jesus said that we would do much greater works than He would (John 14:12). Yet, the requirement is that we believe. The same process that Jesus used to feed the 5000 is the same process we must use to receive our healing. Regardless of the situation; a lack of money or failing health, God always requires one thing-to believe.

Matthew 9:27-29 (ASV) 27And as Jesus passed by from thence, two blind men followed him, crying out, and saying, Have mercy on us, thou son of David. 28And when he was come into the house, the blind men came to him: and Jesus saith unto them, Believe ye that I am able to do this? They say unto him, Yea, Lord. 29Then touched he their eyes, saying, According to your faith be it done unto you.

Looking at this passage we see the two most important statements: "Believe ye that I am able to do this?" and "According to your faith be it done unto you". Jesus is checking out the faith level of these two blind men. The question becomes do we believe that Jesus is able to do this? This question may be applied to many situations and circumstances. Do we believe He is able to heal our bodies, heal our minds, and mend our broken relationships? Can our faith rise to that level? And if it cannot, then we must ask ourselves why.

Do we trust God? Can we truly say we know and love Him, but yet not trust Him? Think about that. Imagine being married to someone who says, "I love you but I don't trust you." This statement is an obvious contradiction. In His Word He says that perfect love will destroy fear (I John 4:17-19). With that in mind, how can fear and love abide in the same place? If we believe that He loves us, why can't we believe that he is able to do this? Whatever your "this" is, isn't God able? Now don't forget the second statement, "According to your faith be it done unto you". This is one of the most powerful statements found in the bible. As believers, we overlook this statement. For instance, there are times in our lives in which all of us either suffer from some type of short-term or long- term illness or we know of someone who is suffering. What do you do when your body is failing to operate according to God's design? Do we complain, or do we begin to confess God's Word by faith, expecting a healing? If we are to study the scriptures we would find that when Jesus miraculously healed the people of God, it was because they expected a miracle. Let us take a look at an event in history in which Jesus demonstrated His healing power.

When Jesus was found in Capernaum, He was told about a captain or a man called a centurion. This captain sought out a healing for his servant.

Take a look at this event in Luke chapter 7:

Luke 7:6-10 (ASV) 6And Jesus went with them. And when he was now not far from the house, the centurion sent friends to him, saying unto him, Lord, trouble not thyself;
for I am not worthy that thou shouldest come under my roof: 7wherefore neither thought I myself worthy to come unto thee: but say the word, and my servant shall be healed.
8For I also am a man set under authority, having under myself soldiers: and I say to this one, Go, and he goeth; and to another, Come, and he cometh; and to my servant, Do this, and he doeth it. 9And when Jesus heard these things, he marvelled at him, and turned and said unto the multi- tude that followed him, I say unto you, I have not found so great faith, no, not in Israel. 10And they that were sent, returning to the house, found the servant whole.

This passage is a great example of a man with great expectations. Not only did the centurion activate his faith in Jesus' healing power, but also the centurion activated his faith for his servant. This is faith in action. The centurion believed that the Lord was so powerful, that He only needed to send the Word and His servant would be healed. We can take a lesson from this man of God. Notice the phrase in verse 7; "But say the word, and my servant shall be healed." This is a statement in which there is a confident expectation that the Lord's Word is powerful. What was the result? The servant of the centurion was found whole. But most of all, the most exciting statement is that Jesus "marveled at him". Just to know that the Lord will marvel at us when we activate our faith is rewarding enough. There is one other fact that we must not overlook; this man was not a man of Israel. This demonstrates that Jesus was given to the entire world.

John3:16 states "For God so loved the world, that He gave His only begotten Son…" Jesus came to demonstrate His glory to the world, not a select few. He came to demonstrate His healing power to the world, not a select few. To what degree we experience His power lies within us. For He said,

Ephesians 3:20-21 (ASV) 20Now unto him that is able to do exceeding abundantly above all that we ask or think, according to the power that worketh in us, 21unto him be the glory in the church and in Christ Jesus unto all generations for ever and ever. Amen.

God is able to do everything. But the extent to which we see His power working in our individual lives depends on our faith in action. He can exceed our expectations. He can exceed what you ask or think. But it hinges on one thing- "according to the power that worketh in you." Take a look at this verse in the Message translation.

Ephesians 3:20-21 (The Message)
20-21God can do anything, you know—far more than you could ever imagine or guess or request in your wildest dreams!

Your Faith and Your Healing

He does it not by pushing us around but by working within us, his Spirit deeply and gently within us.

> **Glory to God in the church!**
> **Glory to God in the Messiah, in Jesus! Glory down all the generations!**
> **Glory through all millennia! Oh, yes!**

It is by His Spirit that the power comes alive in us. We activate that power by using our faith. We use our faith by having great expectations of God.

There is one more important fact revealed by God in Luke7. The Centurion recognized the authority of Jesus. He recognized that Jesus had a heavenly host of soldiers under His command. This is evident when the centurion replied- "I also am a man". The centurion was able to see that Jesus had authority in a spiritual realm unseen to the naked eye. God revealed to Him that Jesus had soldiers under His authority; His heavenly host. The centurion knew what Daniel knew. For in the Old Testament Daniel said in a vision:

As my vision continued that night, I saw someone like a son of man coming with the clouds of heaven. He approached the Ancient One and was led into his presence. 14 He was given authority, honor, and sovereignty over all the nations of the world, so that people of every race and nation and language would obey him. His rule is eternal—it will never end. His kingdom will never be destroyed. (Daniel 7:13-14)

The centurion was confident in His Word. He was confident in His power. Now the point is, do we recognize His authority in our lives? We need to model the centurion. We need to petition God, place our request before him, and have faith in His ability to deliver us. Not just faith, but unwavering faith. For He said in James 1:5-7,

"But when you ask him, be sure that your faith is in God alone. Do not waver, for a person with divided loyalty is as unsettled as a wave of the sea that is blown and tossed by the wind. 7 Such people should not expect to receive anything from the Lord." (NLT)

The Lord is looking for the faith of the centurion in us. He is looking for unwavering faith. He is looking for the power working on the inside of us. The type of power and faith that says, "Just say the Word", and I know my situation will change. "Just say the Word Jesus," and I know I will receive my healing. "Just say the Word Jesus", and I know my breakthrough is coming". Just say the Word Jesus, and I know I will be whole. We will benefit by starting today; expecting God to move, expecting Him to heal, expecting Him to deliver.

Let us take a moment and examine one other person recorded in the Bible. Let us look at a woman of faith who is nameless in the Bible, Matthew 15:21-28:

21 Then Jesus left Galilee and went north to the region of Tyre and Sidon. 22 A Gentile woman who lived there came to him, pleading, "Have mercy on me, O Lord, Son of David! For my daughter is possessed by a demon that torments her severely." 23 But Jesus gave her no reply, not even a word. Then his disciples urged him to send her away. "Tell her to go away," they said. "She is bothering us with all her begging."24 Then Jesus said to the woman, "I was sent only to help God's lost sheep—the people of Israel." 25 But she came and worshiped him, pleading again, "Lord, help me!" 26Jesus responded, "It isn't right to take food from the children and throw it to the dogs." 27 She replied, "That's true, Lord, but even dogs are allowed to eat the scraps that fall beneath their masters' table." 28 "Dear woman," Jesus said to her, "your faith is great. Your request is granted." And her daughter was instantly healed.

Your Faith and Your Healing

Although at first glance it appears hard to receive the harsh reply from the Lord, we must look beyond to see His heart. Jesus fully intended on healing this woman's daughter. Let's examine her steps. First, this Gentile woman approached Jesus, *expecting* a healing, otherwise, why would she bother? Secondly, she was faced with opposition from Jesus' followers. Thirdly, at first the Lord appears to deny her request. He responded with "not even a word". But notice her faith. It says that she "worshiped Him". The woman was diligent in her request. At that moment she had two options: leave discouraged by the Lord's response, or diligently persist in her request. Thankfully, the Gentile woman persisted. She knew that Jesus had the authority on earth to cast out demons. Just like the centurion, she knew, that the power of Jesus is beyond what we can comprehend. She knew within herself "I have a need, and I just met the Man who is the "need meeter" (excuse the English).

This woman knew well the grace and mercy of the Lord. She understood John 3:16. She understood that the healing was not for the house of Israel alone, but for someone of her background. She understood- "that God so loved the world", which included herself and her daughter. Once again, look at the result. What did Jesus say? He said, "Your faith is great – your request is granted". That is what we are looking for; we want the Lord to say, "Your faith is great – your request is granted". However, there are prerequisites. There may be times in our lives in which situations arise, and we must have the faith of the centurion. We petition the Lord, believe in His power, and know that our deliverance is on the way. Yet there are other times in our lives in which we must have the faith of the Gentile woman. The kind of faith that pushes past the obstacles. The kind of faith that recognizes, that God can deliver us. The kind of faith that approaches the throne with boldness, and expects His mercy and grace. The kind of faith that says, "God, I know I am not worthy, but if I can just get a crumb from Your table, I know that all will be well". The Father alone can do it. He alone can heal, deliver, and set us free. As we set our expectations in Him, and petition Him boldly, then and only then, we wait to hear, "your faith is great, your request has been granted."

Chapter 4

FAITH AND YOUR FINANCES

Your request has been granted. This is something we all want to hear from the Father. But when you consider faith, it is important that we remember that faith must be applied. We have seen how faith works for healing. But now, we must see how faith may be applied in our finances. What do you do when you have more bills than you have money? Who do you call when the lights are turned off? How can you be certain that you can afford to give your children a healthy meal daily? The answer may be found in four words -"Have faith in God". The simple fact is, Jesus Christ was our Master Teacher. We can learn from His example. Let's take a minute and follow in His steps. When there was a food shortage, what did He do? The scriptures tell us, He looked toward heaven, blessed what He had in the natural, and spoke by faith to feed 5,000, with two fish and five loaves of bread (see Matthew14). Now let's not move to fast. Look at the action words in this scripture; "looking toward heaven and blessed." How is the word blessed defined in this scripture? Here is the Greek definition according to Strong's Concordance:

1) to invoke blessings
2) to consecrate a thing with solemn prayers
3) to ask God's blessing on a thing
4) pray God to bless it to one's use
5) pronounce a consecratory blessing on

So what lesson can we learn from Christ? When Jesus recognized there was a shortage in the natural, he demonstrated on earth how to mix His earthly resources with His heavenly resources. Remember faith is based on the unseen (Hebrews 11:1). Jesus saw with His spiritual eye the heavenly supply- "He looked toward Heaven." That is where we will also find our supply. We just need to remember to look toward heaven. When Jesus blessed the meal, He took what appeared to the natural eye as a shortage and pronounced a blessing.

He then invoked, consecrated and asked the Father; and His blessing produced an overflow.

This is faith with demonstration. Your mouth must connect you to your faith in God. Jesus didn't go looking for enough, He declared more than enough. So what should we do in a shortage? We must look toward heaven, mix our earthly supply with our heavenly supply, open our mouths by faith, and invoke a blessing. Then you will see twelve basketfuls left over (Luke 9:17). This is the demonstration of Jehovah Jireh, the Lord our provider, Maker of Heaven and earth. He longs to demonstrate His power through us. He is just looking for someone with enough faith to open his or her mouths, and invoke a blessing. Make a commitment today, recognize that the money in the bank that you see, is not all that you have. There is a heavenly supply waiting for you to invoke a blessing. Don't depend on your natural eye. We must open our eyes that we might see (2 Kings 6:17).

Opening our spiritual eyes can be hard if they have been closed for a while. But what did Jesus say? In the book of John, Jesus said that "I came that they may have life, and have that life more abundantly" (John 10:10). In this scripture we all may interpret the word "life" differently. What did Jesus imply when He stated the word life? This scripture indicates that Jesus is referring to everything that you can think of that involves your life. Not only your life here on this earth, at this time, but your life eternally. We will however, focus on your life here on earth. That life consist of your relationships, health, possessions, finances, and spiritual well-being. In 3 John 1:2

How truly I love you! We're the best of friends, and I pray for good fortune in everything you do, and for your good health—that your everyday affairs prosper, as well as your soul! (Message Translation)

This scripture gives us a good indication of the total life. If you take a moment and combine these two scriptures you could actually think of John 10:10 like this,

I came that you may have good fortune in everything you do, good health, blessed and prosperous, and that your soul may increase in Me – and by the way, I came that you have all of this in abundance.

Now, focus on 1/3 of 3 John 1:2. Concentrate on the phrase "everyday affairs prosper". Jesus said that He came that we may have these things in abundance. When you look at the Greek derivative of the word abundance, ***perissos***,

Strong's Exhaustive Concordance defines it as:

1) exceeding some number or measure or rank or need
2) over and above, more than is necessary, superadded
3) exceeding abundantly, supremely
4) something further, more, much more than all, more plainly
5) superior, extraordinary, surpassing, uncommon
6) preeminence, superiority, advantage, more eminent, more remarkable, more excellent

It helps to focus on a few of those words. Take a look at these words: ***exceeding need, over and above, superadded, superior, uncommon, more excellent, and more remarkable. Jesus came that we may have a life that is more excellent, over and above, superior in all respects, and most of all remarkable.*** So we could plainly say that He did not come for us to be in lack, struggling, defeated, and living in a constant deficit. When we take a look at our lives can we say that we are living the life that Jesus intended? We were created as kings and priests, but do our lifestyles testify to that fact? (1 Peter 2:9) Unfortunately most of us are worried, stressed, and strung out concerning overdue bills, escalating living expenses, and sometimes-greedy lifestyles. This is contrary to His will for our lives.

With all the teaching in the Christian culture concerning prosperity, it seems as though only a few people are actually prospering. It seems we may need to examine the disconnection. Why are we not manifesting the lives Jesus came to give us? The answer is, this too comes by faith. What happens when we have more bills than money or more financial responsibilities than our jobs can afford?

We must do one thing-look to the Father. We must look to Him by faith and ask Him for wisdom and knowledge. Just as we look to Father for everything else in the Kingdom, we must look to Him for our needs. If we take a look at one of His basic teachings, Jesus Christ teaches us to pray for our daily needs. This is found in His teaching on prayer. In the Lord's Prayer it states, "Give us this day our daily bread" (Matthew 6:11). The first step in having our needs met daily is to set our day by asking the Father to provide for our daily needs. Notice, He did not teach us to ask for our needs next week, but to take one day at a time, and focus on today's needs. When we look too far ahead, we can create a sense of anxiety within us. He instructs us to be anxious for nothing and do not become overly concerned about tomorrow. "In that one day, you will experience a sufficient amount of challenges (Matthew 6:34)." So, in faith we are to believe we received when we ask (Mark 11:24).

If we were to look into the Old Testament, you would find that God instituted the daily concept of provision. When the Israelites were in the wilderness, God gave them specific instructions on how to collect their provision of manna, In Exodus 16:4-5:

4 Then the LORD said to Moses, "Look, I'm going to rain down food from heaven for you. Each day the people can go out and pick up as much food as they need for that day. I will test them in this to see whether or not they will follow my instructions. 5 On the sixth day they will gather food, and when they prepare it, there will be twice as much as usual." (NLT)

The Lord looks to see if we can pass the test. He is looking to see whether we believe Him to provide for us daily. Notice the phrase "pick up as much food as they need for that day". This is consistent with Jesus' teaching, "Give us our daily bread". Sometimes we are placed in positions in which our faith must

Faith and Your Finances

be tried. When we cannot see enough provision for tomorrow, can we trust that the Lord will provide just enough for that day? Yes, He is a God of abundance, but in order to tap into that abundant supply we must have faith daily.

Secondly, in addition to asking for our daily needs, it is important that we believe that God has a wealth of riches that will never run out. If we are His children, sons and daughters of God, we must believe that we are "joint-heirs" with Christ (Romans 8:17). First, we must fully understand what an heir is. An heir is someone that is given something not due to his or her own actions, but due to who they are related to. A natural heir is someone who is granted something, merely because of his or her relationship. This concept is also apparent with our Heavenly Father. He sees us as joint-heirs. We are joint-heirs with Christ. His Word says, "He owns the cattle on a thousand hills" (Psalms 50:10). We might also add that He owns the hills too! So it stands to reason, if we ask in faith for our daily needs, and believe that He owns it all, why does it appear as though we are not winning in our financial struggles?

The third step has more to do with our actions. Remember, we know that "faith without works is dead" (James 2:17). Once we ask and recognize that God owns it all, we must then walk our daily lives as if the "request has been granted". If we are walking by faith, then we are not worried. If we believe that the request has been granted, then we must live in that manner. If the light bill is due on Friday, then Monday through Thursday, you ought to have sweet sleep (Proverbs 3:24). In other words, live like God said "yes!" One thing that is true about God, if He does not grant our request, we will know.

Now, it is important to insert an important fact here. Yes, God will honor our requests that fall in line with His will, but this does not neglect our personal duties. We must still work and do the best we can with the gifts we are given from God to take care of our responsibilities. The issue is that we recognize that God is always there on our behalf. He is like our Divine vitamin supplement. It is our duty and common sense to make sure that we eat, but vitamins provide the supplemental nutrition we need to physically be well. He is with us on our jobs to make sure that we are the best at what we do, but you have to first show up for work. He is there to give us the knowledge we need to complete a specific task. He is also there to encourage us, when we feel like giving up (Isaiah 41:13-14). The point is, God is always there. His Spirit is within us to comfort, teach, and encourage us to win. His Spirit is there to teach us and guide us. He wants to be glorified through us, and our accomplishments here on earth. It is as simple as this- He is a friend that sticks closer than a brother.

Chapter 5

FAITH FOR OUR RELATIONSHIPS

Who is your best friend? We know that Christ is our friend. He is our friend who laid down His life for us. But how did this great sacrifice impact our earthly relationships? Since we are talking about faith, what is the point of faith, if it does not impact our earthly relationships? Faith in finances is good, and faith for your health is even better, but what about our brothers and sisters in Christ? Sometimes our faith is challenged the most in our relationships. What do you do when you have a child that is distant and does not want to be a part of the family? What about the close friend who just broke your heart? What do you do, when the spouse you love professes to no longer love you? No one has the single solution, but let us take a look at how faith may be used in our relationships.

If we re-visit the biblical definition of faith, we see that "faith is the substance of things hoped for, the evidence of things not seen" (Hebrews 11:1). If your relationships are failing, you need help. In the book of Luke, chapter 15, Jesus teaches a parable about a lost son. First, we have a son that leaves the home without the blessing of his father. Although his father honors his request, the son leaves home prematurely. Secondly, the son proves to be wasteful, unprepared, and lacking good sense. After facing famine and lack, he finally comes to his senses and returns home, but the biggest issue here is the reaction of the father. Although the father knew that the son was probably making mistake, it took faith to believe that he would one day return home. Most parents may not have had the same reaction. But it appears that the father had a quiet peace that his son would one day return.

Luke 15:22-24 (MSNT) 22"But the father said to his servants, "'Fetch a good coat quickly—the best one—and put it on him; and bring a ring for his finger and shoes for his feet. 23Fetch the fat calf and kill it, and let us feast and enjoy ourselves; 24for my son here was dead and has come to life again: he was lost and has been found.' "And they began to be merry.

Here we see a father not only operating in faith, but in love and forgiveness. The father was "hoping" for his son's return.

Well, one thing for sure, we can see faith in this parable. But let us take a look at one of the greatest relationships in the history of the world-the relationship between the Father and the Son. The relationship between the Father and the Son, is the greatest demonstration of faith in relationships.

Jesus Christ-God's only begotten Son (John 3:16), came to this world believing in God who sent Him here to die for the world. In every account of Jesus' life, we see unmovable faith regarding the Father. Christ knew His purpose. Christ knew His Father's good intentions toward Him. In examining His life, one aspect that is interesting is that He came in the form of a man, born of a Virgin, and the Holy Spirit. This is important to keep in mind, because it demonstrates that He had the same challenges and concerns that we have had in our lives (Hebrews 4:15). Yet, Christ walked this earth fully relying and trusting in a faithful God that would never leave or forsake Him. Christ knew that He was sent to this world to die for the sins of mankind, and yet, He had full assurance and faith, that His heavenly Father would resurrect Him from the grave. Think about it. Could you make an agreement to die for the sins of the world and have full assurance that God would raise you from the dead? Take a moment and read this:

Luke 22:39-44 (MSNT) 39 On going out, He proceeded as usual to the Mount of Olives, and His disciples followed Him. 40But when He arrived at the place, He said to them, "Pray that you may not come into temptation." 41But He Himself withdrew from them about a stone's throw, and knelt down and prayed repeatedly, saying, 42"Father, if it be Thy will, take this cup away from me; yet not my will but Thine be done!" 43And there appeared to Him an angel from Heaven, strengthening Him; 44while He—an agony of distress having come upon Him—prayed all the more with intense earnestness, and His sweat became like clots of blood dropping on the ground.

This demonstrates Christ also has shared in our weak moments. Only faith can cause you to say; "Yet not my will but Thine be done!" In His darkest moment, Christ himself knew without a doubt, that the Father's will was most important. This took great faith, great trust, great love and great belief. Jesus Christ said,

John 16:31-33 (MSNT) 31"Do you at last believe?" replied Jesus. 32"Remember that the time is coming, nay, has already come, for you all to be dispersed each to his own home and to leave me alone. And yet I am not alone, for the Father is with me. 33"I have spoken all this to you in order that in me you may have peace. In the world you have affliction. But keep up your courage: I have won the victory over the world."

Faith for Our Relationships

Jesus Christ new that although his closest companions would abandon Him, that God would never leave Him alone. He knew that He had the "victory over the world". Throughout His suffering and crucifixion, He knew that God was there. That one day He would sit on His throne, at the right hand of God, reigning forever.

Christ came to demonstrate to us God's glory and power. He came to show us that we could have faith. He came to show us, that life does not consist in merely those things we can see, but that life consists more in the things we do not see. He knew that God had set His seal on Him, and that the Father would never fail. Christ is our teacher, and we must look to Him for every example in our lives (Luke 6:40). There is no greater challenge than this: to believe in a faithful God, to the point of death. When you take a look around, what other option do we have? We have to believe. When your spouse says that they no longer love you; believe God. When your child leaves home, unprepared and out of touch; believe God. When you feel alone, and it seems as though no one cares; believe God. When you think about it, what is the alternative?

Let's consider the other alternative. What happens if you don't have faith? It will take you only one place-down the road of unbelief, doubt, worry and anxiety. Who has time for that? In reality, everything we are believing for may not materialize in the way we think it should. Or better yet, maybe we are waiting for the right timing of God. It is possible that we will not understand the reason that our prayers did not turn out the way we believed, or for some reason taking longer than we hoped for. But one thing you can count on-when we believe God, He is pleased. That is enough of a reason to believe Him for everything.

God is looking for someone to believe Him, someone who has the kind of faith that can move mountains, someone who can speak to a fig tree (Mark 11). Someone who can heal the sick, deliver the oppressed, and set the captive free. Can we rise to the occasion, or is this kind of faith a thing of the past? Was this faith only for Abraham, Isaac, Jacob, Sarah, Moses, Daniel, Elijah, or some of the other great prophets, men, and women of God? Believers are supposed to be priesthood, a holy nation, a peculiar people (1 Peter 2:9).

Does our faith make us peculiar, or do we live just as the world lives, according to what we can see, touch taste or feel? It is time to take our faith to another level. Time to risk living by the status quo-a time to take God at His Word. He is faithful, and true God. He is the Creator of the universe. He is the One who gives us our breath each day. He is God who spoke and all things came into existence. He is God who gave His Son to die on the cross, and bear the sins of the world. He is God who saves us each day by His compassion, grace and mercy. How can we not take Him at His Word? Let Him heal you, deliver you and mend your relationships. Let Him restore your relationships. Let Him give you peace in the midst of your storms. Just like Jesus, we need to believe. We need the unwavering faith that says, no matter what, "I am not alone". Regardless of the outcome, "Thy will be done". This is faith. This is a life of faith. This is a life pleasing to the Father. This will result in "Well done thy good and faithful servant…enter thou into the joy of the Lord" (Matthew 25:23). Just stand by and expect the Lord to work on your behalf. If you yield your life circumstances to Him, He will be there to see you through. Do you remember Isaiah 41:10?

Chapter 6

FAITH AND ETERNITY

Now most of the discussion has concentrated on the effect of faith during our lifetime on earth. Yet, the most important question is how will our faith impact us eternally? From His Word we can see that our level of faith on earth, can truly impact the quality of our lives. But how does our faith impact us eternally? One question that Jesus states comes to mind:

Mark 9:19 (ASV) 19And he answereth them and saith, O faithless generation, how long shall I be with you? How long shall I bear with you? We must face the fact that living here on earth reflects only one portion of our life. If we don't lose track of the big picture, we can clearly see that the life we live here is merely temporary, just as it was temporary for Jesus. But it is ironic that how we temporarily live our lives, will impact us eternally. With that in mind, one could assume that our level of faith that we demonstrate on earth, will determine our rewards in Heaven and to which level we please our Heavenly Father. Take a look at this scripture:

Matthew 25:14-30 (ASV) 14For it is as when a man, going into another country, called his own servants, and delivered unto them his goods. 15And unto one he gave five talents, to another two, to another one; to each according to his several ability; and he went on his journey. 16Straightway he that received the five talents went and traded with them, and made other five talents. 17In like manner he also that received the two gained other two. 18But he that received the one went away and digged in the earth, and hid his lord's money. 19Now after a long time the lord of those servants cometh, and maketh a reckoning with them. 20And he that received the five talents came and brought other five talents, saying, Lord, thou deliveredst unto me five talents: lo, I have gained other five talents. 21His lord said unto him, Well done, good and faithful servant: thou hast been faithful over a few things, I will set thee over many things; enter thou into the joy of thy lord. 22And he also that received the two talents came and said, Lord, thou deliveredst unto me two talents: lo, I have gained other two talents. 23His lord said unto him, Well done, good and faithful servant: thou hast been faithful over a few things, I will set thee over many things; enter thou into the joy of thy lord. 24And he also that had received the one talent came and said, Lord, I knew thee that thou art a hard man, reaping where thou didst not sow, and gathering where thou didst not scatter; 25and I was afraid, and went away and hid thy talent in the earth: lo, thou hast thine own. 26But his lord answered and said unto him, Thou wicked and slothful servant, thou knewest that I reap where I sowed not, and gather where I did not scatter; 27thou oughtest therefore to have put my money to the bankers, and at my coming I should have received back mine own with interest. 28Take ye away therefore the talent from him, and give it unto him that hath the ten talents. 29For unto every one that hath shall be given, and he shall have abundance: but from him that hath not, even that which he hath shall be taken away. 30And cast ye out the unprofitable servant into the outer darkness: there shall be the weeping and the gnashing of teeth.

In this passage the Lord teaches this lesson and compares it to the Kingdom of Heaven. There are many lessons we can learn from Jesus' teachings. Typically this passage is used to demonstrate the importance of using our resources wisely, while here on earth. The key here is to correlate our faith to the "talents". Clearly we see that there were three men given different levels of "talents" by their lord. But what are talents?

According to the Greek definition, talents is defined as, a sum of money weighing a talent and varying in different states and according to the changes in the laws regulating currency. Normally this passage is used to demonstrate how we are to give. But remember the phrase "For it is as when…" This is a continuation of Matthew 24, in which Jesus uses the lesson concerning the virgins and the bridegroom to teach the disciples about the Kingdom of Heaven.

The key points in this passage are to remember that each of the servants were given something, and were expected to manifest more than what they were given. In the same light, the Father gave His Son to die for our sins, in order to gain many sons and daughters into His Kingdom (John 12:24). Since we are created in His likeness, He expects the same from our lives. We are all given different abilities, but all of us have the same opportunity to live by faith. Jesus said that all we needed was a "grain of a mustard seed" (Matthew 17:20). In this same verse he responded to the disciples saying, "because of the littleness of your faith". This would indicate that according to Jesus, our faith levels are measured- just like the talents. Just like the three men, the question is, "what are we doing with our faith?" Are we hiding our faith like the last servant? Or are we active with our faith like the first two servants. Notice that the first servant had 5 talents, and the second servant had only 2 talents, yet they were both rewarded. This is true of our faith levels. Some believer may have more faith than others, but the question is not a matter of how much faith, but that we are actively reaping rewards from our faith. Notice the description of the two servants-they were both referred to as "faithful servants". Both

Faith and Eternity

servants after a time period were rewarded with 100% of their resources. Both servants were invited to "enter thou into the joy of thy lord". Remember this entire passage is meant to teach the disciples about the Kingdom of Heaven. Jesus is using this lesson to show believers that we are required to do something with what He has left us. We are not called to hide our faith (Matthew 5:15). We are invited to use our faith in such a way, that our faith demonstrates the glory of God, and His Kingdom. Using our faith in the earth will reap not only earthly rewards, but also future eternal rewards, at a 100% return. We want to hear our Lord and Savior say, "enter thou into the joy of thy lord".

What we must avoid is to end our lives here on earth with the same consequences of the third servant. The third servant is guilty of holding a precious possession out of fear. The third servant lacks "faithfulness". The third servant can only see his temporary circumstances. As far as he is concerned, it may not be worth it to risk what he can see for the unseen. One thing can be said-the third servant did lose his talent. But something greater was lost. He was unable to recognize his gain. He saw his master as a "hard man". If we are not careful, we also can fall into this trap. We have to be careful that we do not fail to see the goodness of God. He said, **Matthew 7:9-11 (ASV) 9Or what man is there of you, who, if his son shall ask him for a loaf, will give him a stone; 10 or if he shall ask for a fish, will give him a serpent? 11If ye then, being evil, know how to give good gifts unto your children, how much more shall your Father who is in heav-**

en give good things to them that ask him? If only the third servant believed this truth. If only we can believe this truth. God is not a "hard man". He is a Father, who longs to give us "good things", we just need to be faithful, and ask.

The lesson that we learn here is not merely a message of the financial gains we can make in this life when we invest, but the Heavenly rewards in our eternal life. What happened to the third servant? The third servant was unique in that he hid his talent. Also, notice where he hid it? In the earth. The third servant was too consumed with what was going on in the earth, to take notice of his possible heavenly reward. Not only was he referred to by his lord as a "wicked and slothful servant", but the scripture states that he was cast out into outer darkness, where there will be weeping and gnashing of teeth. This passage does not indicate that he suffered only financial devastation, but that the third servant would be cast into a place that refers to hell, and total separation from God. We could conjecture to say that to live by faith has greater implications than we realize. That faith is not used to be a tool that merely makes our lives comfortable on earth, but it is a measure or "talent" that God will use to determine our "faithfulness" over many things. Our gifts and resources are merely avenues in which we may demonstrate our faith. We want to be found like the first two servants. We want to enter into the "joy of the Lord", because our faith was used to place us there. Faith places us into the joy of our Lord and Savior. Remember, "without faith, it is impossible to please God" (Hebrews 11:6). Knowing how to use our resources along with our faith is important. But being willing and obedient to use our faith and resources is extremely important. When we transition from this life, and stand before God, it is important that Believers realize, that God will not need our money, use our money, or weigh our money; but He will weigh our faith. Remember, the just shall live by faith.

Chapter 7

FAITH AND THE FIGHT

Now let's take a turn and look at faith through a different lens. Let's take a look at faith from a fighting stance. Faith will not only work to provide us for the things we need here on this earth, faith will enable us to fight. Faith causes us to rise to another level, even when troubles are faced on every side. Slow down and read this powerful verse:

2 Corinthians 4:8-9 (NKJV) 8We are hard-pressed on every side, yet not crushed; we are perplexed, but not in despair; 9persecuted, but not forsaken; struck down, but not destroyed. You see in this world we will have problems. We will have trials, and forces of life that come against us. We will be at times "hard-pressed" on every side. Jesus said that we would have tribulations in this world, but don't worry, He came and overcame the world (John 16:33). As believers and followers of Christ, it is imperative that we know that there are instances in our lives in which living by faith is not just an option but also a need. There is a warrior-like faith that we must possess. This is the kind of faith that believes, in spite of my circumstances, I will stand and see the salvation of the Lord (Exodus 14:13). When we look at the church today, we see a sense of hopelessness - a body of people who have lost their fight. As believers, we can't afford not to believe. It is when we are pressed in on every side that we can let faith rise to its highest level. It is like one person said in the past, "it is not until the olive is crushed, that you see the oil." Faith will cause us to continue, in spite of the pain, in spite of the difficulty, in spite of the discomfort. It will cause you to stand in that evil day (Ephesians 6:13). Who knows when our evil day will arrive? One person's evil day may be defined and shaped differently than another's evil day. It is not the circumstance, as much as it is the level to which we stand.

One of the greatest accounts ever told in the bible is the events concerning Jewish men named, Shadrach, Meshach, and Abednego found in Daniel chapter 3. Here you have three men of God who were men of responsibility and title. King Nebuchadnezzar had appointed these men in positions of leadership over the region of Babylon. Then one day, the enemy shows up. No doubt, satan will always place opposition before believers who are called by God. Satan used other men (most likely jealous, and intimidated men) to place Shadrach, Meshach and Abednego in a compromising position. These men were asked to "fall down and worship" a false god. This was a difficult position to be in. These men found themselves in positions of leadership, but called to go against everything within in them. Did they take a moment and think about their future? Did they think about what would happen to their positions if they did not bow? Actually this was the smallest of their worries. It wasn't merely a loss of position they were faced with; they were faced with the possibility of death. King Nebuchadnezzar issued a decree that anyone who did not bow to the sound of music, would be thrown into a burning furnace. Where did these men get the courage to say?

"O Nebuchadnezzar, we have no need to answer you in this matter. 17If that is the case, our God whom we serve is able to deliver us from the burning fiery furnace, and He will deliver us from your hand, O king. 18But if not, let it be known to you, O king, that we do not serve your gods, nor will we worship the gold image which you have set up." (Daniel 3:16-18) NASB

The answer is faith. These men did not have faith in themselves, but faith in God. This event demonstrates warrior-like faith. This is the kind of faith that says in the face of death, "I will trust God". This is fighting faith. Look back at the scripture, notice that the keyword is "able". These men knew that God is able to deliver. These men knew that God is mighty Jehovah Gibbor (Psalms 24:8), the Lord mighty in battle.

Psalms 24:8 (NKJV)
Who is this King of glory?
The LORD strong and mighty,
The LORD mighty in battle.

But this highest level of faith shown here is not only their belief in God, but also their trust in God. These men, had a "nevertheless" type of faith. It is the kind of faith that says, I am believing you God to deliver me, but just in case you don't, I know you are still able. How awesome it would be if we all could attain to this level of faith. Where would the body of Christ be today if we were to develop the type of faith that says, even if it doesn't turn out the way that I hoped, I trust God. I know He is Jehovah Gibbor. I know He is the "King of glory". I know that when the enemy comes in like a flood, that God will lift up a standard against Him (Isaiah 59:19). To be able to say and know without a shadow of a doubt that Jehovah Eli ("My God"-Matthew 27:46), knows what is best for me (Psalms 18:2).

This type of faith must be developed. There may be only a few that develop this type of faith. To name a few of our past heroes- Stephen, Philip, John the Baptist, Isaac, Moses, Esther, and King David.

Faith and The Fight

We can look to the Bible to find great men and women of faith (Hebrews 11). We can also fast forward to our times and find men and women of God of great faith. There was a young girl, who touched many of our hearts across the nation-her name was Rachel Scott. This is one of the best examples of modern-day warrior like faith. Rachel Scott was a 17-year-old junior at Columbine High School. This terrible day will never be forgotten in this nation. Although one of the most devastating events in our history, this young woman left an example of what is truly means to have faith in God. Rachel was shot multiple times, and before dying her faith was tested. At her death it is reported that the shooter asked if she stilled believed in God, and Rachel responded, "You know I do". Rachel was shot in her head and died at Columbine High School (http://en.wikipedia.org/wiki/Rachel_Scott).

Rachel is one among many who have given their lives for their faith. Rachel trusted in God to the point of death. We can learn a lesson from Rachel, and others like her. Why is it so hard for us to believe God? Why do we walk around in despair over meticulous issues, while others can give their very lives? Have we found ourselves at a place where we have begun to view God as a Santa Claus that provides our every wish and desire, and if not, conclude that it is useless to have faith? Where is our warrior-like faith? Like Jesus, we must have faith that says, "nevertheless, not my will, but thy will be done" (Luke 22:42).

Chapter 8

FAITH AND HIS RIGHTEOUSNESS

Besides warrior-like faith, there is a subject that we must visit. This is the subject of righteousness. There are times in which our fight is external as mentioned previously, but what about when our fight is internal? What do we do with those voices within that seem at times difficult to defeat? As we progress through life, all of us hear many voices. Voices within mainstream America are often the loudest; cable television, cell phones, Internet, movies, radio, music, and the list goes on and on. Those are what we call external voices.

What about those silent voices that we have heard over our lifetime? For some of us, this voice is an abusive voice from the past that says, "you will never be good enough", or "you are incapable". Sometimes there are voices that we have created that come from our striving to constantly "measure up". Although very silent at times, those voices must be recognized and dealt with. As believers, we may find ourselves trying to "measure up" in God. In walking as Christians, a true man or woman of God lives to please Him. We are raised in the Word, and strongly encouraged to live our lives according to God's guidelines. We begin our Christian walk, by learning and obeying God's commands. Most of us begin by laying a foundation by learning the Ten Commandments and the rewards and penalties of God's laws. But most of us have realized by now, that we will fail. Sometimes we make decisions, and perform actions that don't please God. So what does faith have to do with it? It is important that as we develop who we are in Christ, that we have the faith to believe that on this journey we walk in the righteousness of Christ.

Let's consider what the Apostle Paul wrote:

Romans 7:14-25 (TMNT) 14I can anticipate the response that is coming: "I know that all God's commands are spiritual, but I'm not. Isn't this also your experience?" Yes. I'm full of myself—after all, I've spent a long time in sin's prison. 15What I don't understand about myself is that I decide one way, but then I act another, doing things I

Faith and His Righteousness

absolutely despise. 16So if I can't be trusted to figure out what is best for myself and then do it, it becomes obvious that God's command is necessary. 17But I need something more! For if I know the law but still can't keep it, and if the power of sin within me keeps sabotaging my best intentions, I obviously need help! 18I realize that I don't have what it takes. I can will it, but I can't do it. 19I decide to do good, but I don't really do it; I decide not to do bad, but then I do it anyway. 20My decisions, such as they are, don't result in actions. Something has gone wrong deep within me and gets the better of me every time. 21It happens so regularly that it's predictable. The moment I decide to do good, sin is there to trip me up. 22I truly delight in God's commands, 23but it's pretty obvious that not all of me joins in that delight. Parts of me covertly rebel, and just when I least expect it, they take charge. 24I've tried everything and nothing helps. I'm at the end of my rope. Is there no one who can do anything for me? Isn't that the real question? 25The answer, thank God, is that Jesus Christ can and does. He acted to set things right in this life of contradic- tions where I want to serve God with all my heart and mind, but am pulled by the influence of sin to do something totally different.

Here we have one of the greatest men of God detailing His struggle with sin. If we take the time to remember, we cannot forget that Paul (formerly Saul) was a persecutor of the church. He was adamant in making sure that the new Christian theology would not thrive. Nevertheless, God selected a man with his background to speak and teach the Gospel. In order for Paul to accept such a task, he had no other choice than to have faith in the righteousness of Christ. This passage was written after his conversion, and at this point, he still notes a struggle with sin. Paul apparently has issues that he is not proud of. Issues that he expected to go away. Nevertheless, in the midst of being called to preach the gospel, he is still found struggling with sin. At one point he says this about himself:

1 Corinthians 15:9-10 (TMNT) 9It was fitting that I bring up the rear. I don't deserve to be included in that inner circle, as you well know, having spent all those early years trying my best to stamp God's church right out of existence.
10But because God was so gracious, so very generous, here I am. And I'm not about to let his grace go to waste. Haven't I worked hard trying to do more than any of the others? Even then, my work didn't amount to all that much. It was God giving me the work to do, God giving me the energy to do it.

Paul has no other choice but to believe in the righteousness of Christ. He said " I am not about to let His grace go to waste". What a statement! His response was "I've tried everything and nothing helps…The answer, thank God, is that Jesus Christ can and does". The Apostle Paul understands that only faith in the righteousness of Christ allows him to stand, and be committed to his call. The Apostle did not feel worthy enough to be called to the cause of Christ. His faith in the righteousness of Jesus is what allowed him to extend

Faith and His Righteousness

his viewpoint beyond what he thought of himself. He was able to view himself the way God viewed him. What does that mean for us today? Simple. God does not want us to fulfill our mission and answer our call based on our view of our worthiness, but on His worthiness.

As we live in this sin-fallen world, we will have struggles. We will have inner issues that try to pull us toward sin. There will be times in our lives in which we make mistakes. But we are called to respond like Paul and state, "I'm not about to let His grace go to waste". We must however be cautious. Does that mean that we sin intentionally, and abuse His grace? No. There is a place in God that when a true conversion takes place, that sin in our lives will begin to grieve us. A believer, who has had a true conversion, does not seek to displease the Father. We all may make the wrong choices and perform the wrong actions, but the sin that we must be aware of, is the practice of sinning. We have often heard the statement, "Don't grieve the Holy Spirit". The Holy Spirit is grieved when we practice sin, and have no intentions in our heart to correct ourselves and repent. We grieve the Spirit of God when we participate willingly with the works of the devil through our flesh. In I John 3, it says,

1 John 3:8 (TMNT) 8Those who make a practice of sin are straight from the Devil, the pioneer in the practice of sin. The Son of God entered the scene to abolish the Devil's ways. Notice the last part of the scripture-"the Son of God entered the scene to abolish the Devil's ways." When we find our- selves struggling to serve God in our own righteousness, it is at that time that we must have faith in God. We must look at and remember the cross. This is where Jesus "finished the work" (John 4:34). At the cross is where Jesus offered an exchange. He exchanged our righteousness for His righteousness. By faith we access the righteousness of Jesus Christ.

If you are not convinced, consider one more great man of God-Peter. Peter was always on the front line, ready and willing to accept the challenges posed by Jesus. But even Peter had inner struggles. Peter was the one who said,

Mark 14:29 (TMNT) 29Peter blurted out, "Even if everyone else is ashamed of you when things fall to pieces, I won't be."

Peter did the very thing that he believed he wouldn't do- he denied Christ. On the night that Christ was betrayed, Peter denied Him three times. After following Christ so closely, this had to be difficult for Peter. But what happened to Peter? After this event, Peter was extremely sorrowful concerning his denial. At this point Peter had two options. Peter could fall into severe depression and condemnation, or by faith, accept God's grace and walk in the righteousness of Christ. Peter chose the second option. The scriptures state that after the crucifixion of Christ, Peter was found among the disciples (Mark 16:7). Actually, Peter was one of the first to run ahead to the tomb and discover that the tomb was

Faith and His Righteousness

empty. Peter realized something very important. He realized that his mission for Christ was greater than his guilt. Peter like Paul truly knew that the righteousness of Christ was available to him.

So what is the big deal? Well, most of us will not find ourselves in a situation like Peter where we walked with Christ then denied him, or persecuted the church like Paul. So if these great men of God needed the righteousness of Christ, don't we? Like Peter and Paul we must have faith in the righteousness of Christ. We must remember that there is no condemnation for those who are in Christ (Romans 8:1). We must remember that it is not what is in us that will make us right, but what is right in Him.

This is the wonderful message of the Cross- God is righteous and He is good (Mark 10:18). So what does that have to do with faith? Well the issue is that He is good, and there is nothing we can do about it, but believe. One of the most important realizations as a Christian is to remember the goodness of God. Through His goodness He has redeemed us from the curse of death, and has caused us to be reconciled to Him through His Son Jesus Christ (Galatians 3:13). God is so good that He sent his only begotten Son to die for us on the cross. Yes, God is good. So how does that truth translate to our daily lives? This in fact is the cornerstone of our lives. Where most believers go wrong is that they fail to have faith in His goodness-His supreme goodness. From the very beginning God created us to be in fellowship with Him (Genesis 1:26-27). The very first action that God did for Adam and Eve was to bless them (verse 28). According to Strong's concordance, one of the definitions of bless is "to adore". It is exciting to know that once God created us, he wanted us to know that He adored us. But the question is do we believe that? Do we have faith in His adoration for us? Why is it so hard to accept, when at the same time we know that he died for us? God's ways are good. His thoughts toward us are good. He said, "For I know the thoughts that I think toward you, saith the LORD, thoughts of peace, and not of evil, to give you an expected end" (Jeremiah 29:11). Take a look at these same verses, and a few additional in the Message translation

11I know what I'm doing. I have it all planned out—plans to take care of you, not abandon you, plans to give you the future you hope for. 12"When you call on me, when you come and pray to me, I'll listen. 13"When you come looking for me, you'll find me. "Yes, when you get serious about finding me and want it more than anything else, 14I'll make sure you won't be disappointed." GOD's Decree

Notice the last two words -"God's Decree". That means that God will not change His mind. It is settled. He has issued forth a royal statement straight from His throne. He is telling His family, don't worry, don't fret, I am a good God. I watch out over you and the affairs of your life because you belong to me. "I will make sure you are not disappointed".

Faith and His Righteousness

Although we may not understand everything, we must settle in our lives that God is on our team, if we let Him be the captain. He will call the best moves to get us to win the game. Just like a football team, He will block if necessary, call us in for a huddle, or sometimes advise us to sit out on the bench. Regardless of His call, we must have faith that the call He makes is intended for us to win the game. He doesn't play to lose. We must remember that the game is fixed. If we follow His game plan, we are guaranteed a win!

Let's face it; we all know that living for God may not be easy. There are things we don't understand or comprehend. There are times when we wonder, "Why did God allow this in my life?" This is when the supernatural faith must kick in. Faith in His goodness, says "I don't understand everything, but I know that His plans for me are good." To believe in His goodness is to believe and know His nature. Right now one important person comes to mind. Let's take a look at what she had to say:

Luke 1:46-54 (KJV) 46And Mary said, My soul doth magnify the Lord, 47And my spirit hath rejoiced in God my Saviour. 48For he hath regarded the low estate of his handmaiden: for, behold, from henceforth all generations shall call me blessed. 49For he that is mighty hath done to me great things; and holy is his name. 50And his mercy is on them that fear him from generation to generation. 51He hath showed strength with his arm; he hath scattered the proud in the imagination of their hearts. 52He hath put

down the mighty from their seats, and exalted them of low degree. 53He hath filled the hungry with good things; and the rich he hath sent empty away. 54He hath holpen his servant Israel, in remembrance of his mercy;

Take a moment and reflect on this statement:

"For he that is mighty hath done to me great things; and holy is his name." God is rich in mercy and He wants to do great things for us. Do we believe in His goodness? God and His goodness cannot be separated. Even in times in which he has allowed destruction, we cannot forget that He is just and good. If He allowed evil ways of man to go unpunished, it would contradict His nature. He is just, and He is good. God is searching for us, to love Him and commit ourselves to Him. We all must be like David and confess that His goodness and mercy will follow us all the days of our lives (Psalm 23).

David was convinced; he said "surely goodness and mercy will follow me all the days of my life." And like David, we must be confident. We must have an expectation of God's goodness in our lives. That He wants to shine His face upon us (Psalm 80:3). God is great, and should be recognized for His greatness and His supreme ability to love us unconditionally. He is faithful to His word. God actually used His creation to remind us of His faithfulness. We have a rainbow placed in the sky, for us to remember that He is faithful to His Word (Genesis 9:13). He is looking for a place in our lives that does not compete for time or attention. He is God alone.

Faith and His Righteousness

He is the "I Am". He is the "Ancient of Days". Knowing this, we can have faith in His goodness-faith in His plans for us, faith that He is waiting for the day in which we will be fully reconciled to Him. Take a moment and read one of the most poetic scriptures is found in Zephaniah 3.

Zephaniah 3:17 (KJV) 17The LORD thy God in the midst of thee is mighty; he will save, he will rejoice over thee with joy; he will rest in his love, he will joy over thee with singing.

What other reason is there to rejoice? It is good to know that our God, will save. Our God will rejoice over us. Our God will rest in His love for us. Our God will joy over us with singing! We have to be convinced at this point. God is good; we just have to believe in His goodness.

Chapter 9

FAITH AND HIS LOVE

Now let's challenge ourselves further. Hopefully you are convinced at this point that God is good, but what about His love? Do you truly believe that God loves you? Most of us believe that God is love, and that He is loving, but do we accept and receive the love He has for us? Do we have the faith and belief that He truly loves us? The entire universe, all that we see is a direct result of His affection and love towards mankind. His Word states, "For God so loved the world that He gave His only begotten Son, that whosoever believeth in Him should not perish but have everlasting life" (John 3:16). One of the most important words in this scripture is one of the shortest- it is the word "so". God not only loves us, He "so" loves us. If you can imagine this try and believe that God loved us so much that even the Heavens could not contain His love. He created another entity just to express His love towards us, and called it earth. In the beginning He said, "Let us create man in our own image and likeness…" (Genesis 1:26)

Not only through creating the earth does God demonstrate His love, but also throughout time, God has used several events to display His love towards mankind. The most commonly remembered events are the challenges that the Israelites faced thousands of years ago. The Israelites were God's chosen people. Take a moment and recall their life in the wilderness. The Israelites were held captive by the Egyptians, and God used Moses, a special man of God to help deliver the Israelites. Take a look at Exodus 3:6-10 from the Message translation,

6Then he said, "I am the God of your father: The God of Abraham, the God of Isaac, the God of Jacob." Moses hid his face, afraid to look at God. 7 GOD said, "I've taken a good, long look at the affliction of my people in Egypt. I've heard their cries for deliverance from their slave masters; I know all about their pain. 8And now I have come down to help them, pry them loose from the grip of Egypt, get them out of that country and bring them to a good land with wide-open spaces, a land lush with milk and honey, the land of the Canaanite, the Hittite, the Amorite, the Perizzite, the Hivite, and the Jebusite. 9"The Israelite cry for help has come to me, and I've seen for myself how cruelly they're being treated by the Egyptians. 10It's time for you to go back: I'm sending you to Pharaoh to bring my people, the People of Israel, out of Egypt."

In this passage God is demonstrating His love for His people. He identifies Himself as "The God of your father..." God is in Heaven on His throne, but He is never far away from His people. Notice the term in verse 7, *"My people"*. God knows and has identified us as *His people*. He watches over us faithfully and can see every distress and heartache in our lives. He is never absent. He knows "our pain." Our cries come to Him in the middle of the night and during the early part of the day; God hears our cries. "He sees for himself." Notice in the scripture it states in verse 8, *"And now I have come down to help them..."* It is nice to know that God will come down to help us. We must know that He has sent His Holy Spirit to help us (John 14:15:20).

This is love. This is love demonstrated. God is a deliverer. He places men and women in His earth, to bring about His will. But first in order to act, we have to believe He is who He says He is, and undoubtedly believe in His love and care. This love is no longer just for the Israelites. He extended His love to the race of Gentiles. There was a time in which He came to His chosen people only. One of the most challenging verses in the Bible to comprehend is one of the verses mentioned previously.

Take a look again at Matthew 15, beginning with verse 23, *Jesus ignored her. The disciples came and complained, "Now she's bothering us. Would you please take care of her? She's driving us crazy." 24Jesus refused, telling them, "I've got my hands full dealing with the lost sheep of Is-*

rael." 25Then the woman came back to Jesus, went to her knees, and begged. "Master, help me." 26He said, "It's not right to take bread out of children's mouths and throw it to dogs."27She was quick: "You're right, Master, but beggar dogs do get scraps from the master's table." 28Jesus gave in. "Oh, woman, your faith is something else. What you want is what you get!" Right then her daughter became well.

Jesus knew that He came to reveal himself to "the lost sheep of Israel". Here Jesus is demonstrating His love for the world. Notice His last response- "your faith is something else". This woman had to believe in the love of Jesus. She had to believe that Jesus loved her enough to extend His miracle working power to her daughter. It was her faith in His love and mercy that healed her daughter.

God's love for us is indescribable. He formed us and shaped us in His image. There is life in His love. Every breath we take is created from His love. He gives us His breath. He breathes on us each day, the newness of His life, if we will only accept it. He said, that He knew us, before the foundations of the earth. He created us uniquely (Psalm 139). He knew us in our mother's womb. In Jeremiah 1, He was speaking to the prophet, but He is also speaking to us today.

He is saying, "Don't forget that I knew you before. I knew you before the world was formed. I love you and uniquely created you to display my glory in the earth. Do you believe I love you? I have consecrated you for Myself."

Faith and His Love

God's love is a unique gift extended to us throughout eternity. We must grab hold to it, and never let it go. Through the difficult times, challenges, and chaos, we must live this life focused on His love for us. God sent His Son as a sacrifice for us. God has delivered us. God has provided healing for us. His power is available to us. He is not focused on our shortcomings; He is focused on His love for us. Only by faith can you receive His love. Only by faith can you come to His cross. Only by faith, can you lean on His everlasting arm (Deuteronomy 33:27). He is the Alpha and Omega of your life (Revelation 22:13). He began a good work in you, and He is faithful to complete it (I Thessalonians 5:24).

When Jesus hung his head on the cross, He said "It is finished" (John 19:30). What was finished? Yes, He conquered death. Yes, He conquered sin. Yes He conquered the works of satan. But most of all, when He said "It is finished," there at the cross He demonstrated that there is no more doubt. Doubt is finished. He gave His life to show us, that He loved us completely, sacrificially, and fully. He took the nails in His hand, to hold us now in the palms of His hand.

He took the crown on His head, to show us He has given us a new mind, with new thoughts.

He took the nails in His feet, to let us know, "I will never leave you, nor forsake you" (Hebrews 13:5). I will be with you wherever you go. He took the stripes on His back to let you know, everywhere you hurt, I see, and I am there for you.

Whenever you need me in your pain, I am there. He took the spit in His face to show you, I love you so much that I will humble myself for you. Yes, I know that I am a King, but because of my love for you, this spit in my face means nothing. He took being slapped in the face because He needed you to know that there is no pain that I don't understand. He took the spear in His side, just so you would know that where the water is, where the blood is, there you will find your life. Live your life fully in Me. Run to Me, draw close to Me. Where the water is, you will never thirst (John 4:14). Where the blood is I will always forgive. No payment is required. I love you. Unconditionally, I love you. And by the way, my legs were never broken, because I am coming back for you. I am on my throne in heaven, but one day, I am coming back to reclaim you to myself. Remember, "You have been reconciled to Christ".

Galatians 2:20 (KJV) 20I am crucified with Christ: nevertheless I live; yet not I, but Christ liveth in me: and the life which I now live in the flesh I live by the faith of the Son of God, who loved me, and gave himself for me.

Yes, we must all have faith in Jesus Christ and His love for us. He completely and finally demonstrated His love on the cross. There is a wonderful book written by Dr. Ben Lerner titled, ***"Body by God"***. In this book, Dr. Lerner wrote that we must have a "PH.D" in our faith. We must get to a point where we are "past having doubt" in our faith and believe in His love for us. It is finished. It is settled. The Father, the Son, and the Holy Spirit, has cast their love upon us never to be removed.

Faith and His Love

Chapter 10

FAITH IN JESUS CHRIST

Faith in His love is easy when you have faith in who Jesus Christ is. Most believers understand that His death set us free, but what about the resurrected Jesus? When Jesus rose, He took His position in Heaven seated on the right hand of the Father. His ministry and purpose on earth was to destroy the works of the devil. But His greater purpose was accomplished when he restored and reconciled us to the Father. We will live eternally with the Father. But for our present time, we recognize that Jesus Christ established us back into a relationship with the Father. We were once separated from God by the fall that took place in The Garden of Eden. Jesus came as the last Adam, to eternally restore all that the first Adam had abolished. He came in the form of a man so that he could "dwell among us" (Revelation 21:3) He took on the form of man, yet without sin, so that His blood would forever cover those of us who were sinners.

Speaking of Adam, let's take a moment and revisit the account of his children Cain and Abel. If you recall, Cain killed his brother Abel because of resentment. Cain resented the fact that Abel's offering was accepted and his was not. In a fit a rage, Cain struck and killed Abel. Look at this scripture found in Genesis chapter 4:9

Then the LORD said to Cain, "Where is Abel your brother?" He said, "I do not know. Am I my brother's keeper?" 10And He said, "What have you done? The voice of your brother's blood cries out to Me from the ground. 11So now you are cursed from the earth, which has opened its mouth to receive your brother's blood from your hand.

As a result Cain was banished from God's presence and given a mark. What is odd is that God could have chosen to kill Cain. But instead of killing him, God decided instead to banish Cain from His presence. This is very similar to what happened to Adam. God could have chosen to kill Adam and Faith In Jesus Christ

Eve, but instead decided to banish them from his presence. Here you have an innocent man, Abel, who was killed, and another man, Cain, a murderer, allowed to live in spite of his sin. This occurrence demonstrates the power and awesomeness of God's mercy. What is interesting is another scripture that states, "Without the shedding of blood, there is no remission of sins" (Hebrews 9:22). Not just any blood, but innocent blood. Abel's blood was innocent. Look at God's response; He said to Cain "The voice of your brother's blood cries out to Me from the ground." Abel is dead, Cain is separated from the presence of God, and yet the blood is still crying out. What does that have to do with us? Well, if you think about it, we like Cain, were once dead in our trespasses, we were once separated from God, but Jesus' blood cried out on our behalf.

Hebrews 12:24 (YLT) 24and to a mediator of a new covenant—Jesus, and to blood of sprinkling, speaking better things than that of Abel!

It doesn't stop there: His innocent blood is still crying out on our behalf. Every wrong turn we make. Every intentional and unintentional sin, His blood cries out on our behalf. His blood is still working to sanctify us (Hebrews 13:12). It is similar to the mark of Cain. God gave Cain the mark for his protection and declared that anyone who would hurt Cain was guaranteed vengeance from the Lord. Here it is, Cain, deserves to die, but instead receives the protection from the Lord. It is a demonstration of God who is both merciful and just. We must not look at Jesus' death on the cross as a past event but a current event that works on our behalf to this very day, crying out on our behalf. Other than His blood crying out for us day-by-day, moment- by-moment, Jesus has another important role in our lives. He is our great high priest. God made Jesus our great and final high priest. It is important to remember that when we participate in communion, it is as if we are with Him just like the disciples were. Every time we participate in communion Jesus is there by His Spirit, as we do it in remembrance of Him. He is the great High Priest who tore down the veil once and for all that separated us from the Father. He presents Himself as the final sacrifice for our lives.

He today is the final High Priest who has left His word to wash and cleanse our souls. He is the High Priest that serves in God's heavenly tabernacle. Just like the candlesticks in the tent of meeting, He is the light that shines through our lives continually. He is the bread that was once represented by the showbread that was in the tabernacle. He daily feeds us with more of himself like the manna given to the Israelites in the wilderness. He is there as our High Priest at the altar of incense, interceding on our behalf, tending to our prayers and presenting them to the Father as a sweet smelling aroma. Jesus, our great High Priest is still actively working on our behalf. While on earth He said,

John 5:17 (YLT) 17And Jesus answered them, 'My Father till now doth work, and I work;' We must have faith to believe that although He died on the cross, His ministry is not dead. His work was finished at that time on earth. He is not only working now, He will work on our behalf until the end.

He promised us that at some appointed time that He will return for His bride. We are the bride. He will return to the earth and gather those who believed in his name. He will separate the "wheat from the tares" (Matthew 13:29). That is why we pray "thy kingdom come, thy will be done". On that great and terrible day, He will gather us into His kingdom, and once and for all establish His kingdom on earth. And at that time "at the name of Jesus, every knee will bow, and every tongue will confess, that Jesus Christ is Lord"(Romans 14:11). That is the key. Jesus Christ is Lord, whether we accept it or not. He is the King of Kings, whether we believe it or not, and one day will come to rule and reign.

As mentioned earlier He said, "When the Son of Man returns, will He find faith on the earth?" (Luke 18:8) Jesus is coming back for His bride. We have been betrothed to Him. The important question is when He returns; will He find faith in you? Will your faith fail? If the trumpet sounded tomorrow, would you be gathered to reign in His kingdom? He has already proven His love for you. Have you proven your love for Him? Are you crucified with Christ (Galatians 2:20)? Is He the great and High Priest of your life? We have to make sure we keep our priorities straight. That will be the greatest test of faith. The priority is to make sure that our faith stood the test of time. That we did not waiver or stagger at the promise, and we are found faithful to Christ. It is an issue of eternity. The irony is that we have a test within the framework of time that will determine our eternal destiny. We are given only one chance-one life to demonstrate our faithfulness. We don't have an opportunity for multiple attempts. There is only one file of our lives. We are not given the opportunity to delete our life file and save or overwrite it. Whatever is found on the "hard-drive" of our lives, will testify about our love for the risen Savior. It is important that we download a huge file of faith from our Lord and Savior Jesus Christ. We don't need any "bugs" in our faith. It is important that our faith runs without "operator error". We have a great programmer in the heavens who will determine our eternal reward. Will we reign with Christ forever because our faith pleased the Father?

Chapter 11

FAITH IN HIS HOLY SPIRIT

When we first began our walk with the Father, it all began with Jesus Christ (Romans 10:9-10). But what about the Holy Spirit? There are many believers today, who have faith in God, and faith in Jesus, but don't have faith in the Holy Spirit. How can this be when the three are one? The Father, the Son, and the Holy Spirit are all one-the Trinity. This belief is foundational for a Christian. So this is the point; do we have a passive belief concerning the Holy Spirit? Do we "kinda–sorta" believe in Him, yet do not have a relationship with Him? We must have faith in the Holy Spirit. He is the very Spirit of God. The Holy Spirit is who helps us here on earth. If you recall the beginning of Jesus' ministry He was first baptized by John the Baptist, and the Holy Spirit. The scriptures state that the Holy Spirit descended on Him like a dove (Luke 3:22). Jesus demonstrated to us that we must have the Holy Spirit descend on us like a dove in order to have effective ministry in the earth. He told the apostles to wait in the upper room, until they were baptized by the Holy Spirit;

Acts 1:4-5 (NKJV) 4And being assembled together with them, He commanded them not to depart from Jerusalem, but to wait for the Promise of the Father, "which," He said, "you have heard from Me; 5for John truly baptized with water, but you shall be baptized with the Holy Spirit not many days from now."

This was an instruction that was given to the apostles who walked physically with Jesus on the earth. We must understand that the Holy Spirit must be invited to work in our lives (Luke 11:13). He will not force himself on us. He is the "Promise of the Father". It is our faith in Him that allows Him to operate freely in our lives. He is not mystical. He is not magical. He is the very Spirit of God. We just merely need to open our hearts, operate by faith, and ask Him to operate in our lives. It takes time to know Him. It takes time to learn from Him, but if we are willing, He is willing. He is here by faith to "guide us into all truth" (John 16:13).The

Spirit of God is given to us so that we may yield to His will, and work to establish His Kingdom. He is given to us by faith, and has a ministry on earth. Jesus said:

John 14:25-28 (NKJV) 25"These things I have spoken to you while being present with you. 26But the Helper, the Holy Spirit, whom the Father will send in My name, He will teach you all things, and bring to your remembrance all things that I said to you. 27Peace I leave with you, My peace I give to you; not as the world gives do I give to you. Let not your heart be troubled, neither let it be afraid. 28You have heard Me say to you, 'I am going away and coming back to you.' If you loved Me, you would rejoice because I said, 'I am going to the Father,' for My Father is greater than I.

Notice that Jesus referred to the Holy Spirit as your Helper and Teacher. Jesus and the Father are in Heaven. It is the Holy Spirit who was sent to teach us "all things". Without knowing Him, how can we truly know the Father? Without knowing Him, how can we truly know Jesus? We are to rejoice, because Jesus has gone to the Father, yet He has not left us alone. Every day by faith we must seek to know the Spirit of God. Every day we must position ourselves to become acquainted with Him and His ministry. Jesus was with the Holy Spirit at the beginning, and He was with Him at the end. It was the Spirit of God that descended on Jesus at the beginning and it was the Spirit of God that was there at which appeared to be the end.

Romans 8:11 (NKJV) 11But if the Spirit of Him who raised Jesus from the dead dwells in you, He who raised Christ from the dead will also give life to your mortal bodies through His Spirit who dwells in you.

The Spirit of God gives you life. He is the very breath that brings us to life. If you go back to Genesis, you can see that God created Adam, but life did not come until the breath of God was given. This is a strong parallel to the Spirit of God. We can go to church, sing songs, play instruments, but without the Spirit of God giving life to all we do, and breathing on us, whatever we attempt to do will not come to life. We have to believe that without Him, we are not complete. He gives us the breath of life. He gives new life to us. The Father has been working, Jesus is working, and if we allow Him, the Spirit of God wants to work within us. This is not a discussion about the gifts of the Holy Spirit, or even the fruit of the Holy Spirit. This is a discussion about Him. His gentleness, kindness, comfort, compassion, and love for us. He is just waiting on His invitation in our lives to work freely within us. To trust Him enough to be there for us.

Even within ministry we can fall in the trap of satan, and believe that if we pray hard enough, or fast long enough, than we can accomplish God's will. We must understand that it is only through the power and faith in the Holy Spirit that God's will can come to pass in our lives. Faith alone in Him is how we stand. Faith alone in Him is how we fellowship with the Father. We cannot forget His identity. He is our teacher. He is our guide. He is our Comforter. He is our Healer. Without Him, we can't do anything (John 15:5). Jesus gave us an example to follow. He demonstrated it with himself, and He demonstrated the need for the Holy Spirit, through His apostles.

The conclusion of the matter is this; we must believe and have faith in the Holy Spirit, and allow Him to operate freely in our lives. This is a matter of believing and trusting in who He is.

Chapter 12

FAITH IN THE FATHER

Now we know the importance of believing in His Son and in His Holy Spirit, but what about the Father? What does it mean to have faith in the Father? What is it like to trust Him as your caretaker and friend? Faith in the Father, will help us to become the essence of who we are. How can we take our daily breaths each day without believing that He loves and cares for us? In order to have faith in the Father, it is important to go back to the beginning.

In the beginning is where we can see his true intent and purpose for our lives. In the beginning is where we can see why He created us. It is where He establishes His order. It is where He set up His guidelines and conditions. We have to have faith and belief that he knows what is best for us. That He created us for his glory. We must believe that He intimately created us. From His likeness and His image, He set our feet on this earth, and gave us the breath of life. How can we take His breath everyday, moment by moment, and not believe Him for our lives? Why is it so hard to trust Him? What are we missing? Let's take a look at the beginning.

Genesis 1:27-28 (NKJV) 27So God created man in His own image; in the image of God He created him; male and female He created them. 28Then God blessed them, and God said to them, "Be fruitful and multiply; fill the earth and subdue it; have dominion over the fish of the sea, over the birds of the air, and over every living thing that moves on the earth."

It is always helpful to pay attention to the verbs in a passage. Notice the action taken by God. This scripture states that God **created**, and then **blessed**. Let's repeat that. God created then blessed. What else is left? Once He created us, we have to remember that He created us, and then He set every provision necessary for our lives.

Take a look of these definitions of the word bless:

1. To request of God the bestowal of divine favor on
2. To bestow good of any kind upon
(retrieved from www.dictionary.com)
Before we can proceed through studying the bible, we must

first receive this foundational truth- that when we were created God "bestowed" a gift. In our culture most people celebrate their birthdays and receive gifts. Just imagine going to a birthday party and friends and family showering gifts upon you, yet you never get to a point where you open the gifts. God's blessing works in the same fashion. The gift is there; it is just a matter of opening the gift. The gift is accessed by faith. Remember, "God is not a man that He should lie"(Numbers 23:19). If He said, "I have given you a gift" then, that settles it. However, how many of us have gone through our lives carrying the gift, but never truly opening the gift? The gift is accessed by faith. Nothing else will open our gift from God. Wishful thinking will not do. Positive thinking will not do. The only thing that will open our gift is faith in God.

God has set us here on earth at this time to accomplish His "good pleasure". He has enabled us through His blessing, to accomplish His will on earth. But if we walk around, depressed, oppressed and barely getting by, what glory does God receive? If anything, our lives can be used by satan, to show a contradiction. When we look into the eyes or our brothers and sisters, do we see victory or defeat? Do we see the victory that Jesus said, "overcomes the world" (I John 5:4)? Is the world overcoming us? Belief in God and His plans, intentions, and will for our lives are fundamental to living. It is as important as taking our next breath. He gives us air to breathe, eyes to see, legs to walk. In His omnipotence, He has set us in the earth to establish and testify to His goodness. Take a look at one of the most powerful testimonies of who God is found in this passage:

Exodus 3:12-15 (NKJV) 12So He said, "I will certainly be with you. And this shall be a sign to you that I have sent you: When you have brought the people out of Egypt, you shall serve God on this mountain." 13Then Moses said to God, "Indeed, when I come to the children of Israel and say to them, 'The God of your fathers has sent me to you,' and they say to me, 'What is His name?' what shall I say to them?"14And God said to Moses, "I AM WHO I AM." And He said, "Thus you shall say to the children of Israel, 'I AM has sent me to you.'" 15Moreover God said to Moses, "Thus you shall say to the children of Israel: 'The LORD God of your fathers, the God of Abraham, the God of Isaac, and the God of Jacob, has sent me to you. This is My name forever, and this is My memorial to all generations.'

Here, when Moses is asking God for His name, notice His response, "I AM WHO I AM". Take a moment and meditate on that for a moment. Repeat it to yourself audibly, until it is settled in your spirit. What a unique response. At this moment, our Father had every opportunity to respond to Moses with any name. But He chose to respond to Moses, by a name that indicates His character. Think about when someone comes to knock on your door. Some of us may ask, "Who is it?" The person on the other end may respond, "It's me!" Notice, they did not give a specific name, but

Faith In The Father

Faith In The Father

responded by letting you know that when you open the door, you will know without a shadow of a doubt, that the per- son on the other side is whom you expect. You would not open your door for a perfect stranger, or for someone without good intentions. You would only open your door for some- one who you knew was exactly who they said they were, and recognized the sound of their voice. It is the same way with God. God is using this inspired scripture to tell Moses, go to the people and tell them, that I am exactly who I said I was; "I AM WHO I AM". He used that scripture then, and He is still using it today to say to His people "I AM WHO I AM". Take me at my word. Believe Me. When you open the door, expect that it is Me on the other side. Open the door, you know My voice. You just have to believe. Don't see me through your circumstances; expect Me to be con- stantly there, through the good and the bad times.

We must believe that the Father is who He says He is. Who does God say that He is? Well, He says that He is our de- fender, our shield, and our rear guard. He is our overseer, the captain of our ship, the Bishop of our souls. He is the creator of the heavens; Creator of the visible and invisible. He is sovereign, a mighty ruler, conqueror and friend. Who does God say that He is? He is the everlasting Father and the Ancient of Days. He has established His throne in the Heav- ens. He has manifested Himself on the earth as Jesus and the Holy Spirit. He is our strength, our bread of Life. He is love. He is Holy. He is righteous and just. He is the Father who is there. He is the Father who does not slumber or sleep.

He is our water when we are thirsty, our bread when we our hungry, and our friend when we our lonely.

So what do we do? Believe God. Faith in God is not optional it is essential. Faith in God is our foundation. Faith in God establishes us in the earth. Faith in God allows us to be all that He has planned for us to be. Faith in God is not optional, Faith in God is essential. We must increase our faith in Him. He said to Moses, "I AM WHO I AM". He is saying to us, to all generations, do not forget, " I AM WHO I AM".

Knowing and believing God is reward enough. But, He has even more in store for us. When you try to draw a conclusion, we might find ourselves saying, "What is it all for?" What if I believe in God? What if I believe in Jesus? What if I believe in the Holy Spirit? What is it all for? It is for one thing-to have eternal life with the Father, Son, and Holy Spirit. Having faith on earth, leads us into our eternal reward-life eternally, living in His holy Kingdom. The entire journey here on earth, is meant to develop us into the image of His Son. We are called to conform to His image in order to share our lives with Him. His entire purpose was to come to the earth and reconcile us back unto Him. The Father, the Son, and the Holy Spirit, were working together from the beginning to set a plan in motion. That plan was to create an opportunity for us to accept Him as our Lord and Savior, and spend life eternally with the Father. One of the most promising statements from Jesus is heard from the cross. Right before His death, He said, "It is finished"(John19:30).

What was finished? All that He had planned for us, at that moment became settled in Heaven. Jesus Christ came and gave His life so that we could have life in Him. What is it all for? What is faith for? We can conclude that faith is not about our jobs, promotions or comfortable life styles. We can conclude that it is not about our relationships, college education, or even family relationships. We can conclude, that it is not about the money, the fancy vacations, or even the latest vehicles. It is not about our church titles, and our executive offices. It is all about our resurrected lives with Him. Jesus came that we would have life, and have that life more abundantly (John 10:10). It is time to shift our focus. We must turn our eyes back toward Heaven. We must look unto Jesus, the author and finisher of our faith.

Hebrews 12:2 (NKJV) 2looking unto Jesus, the author and finisher of our faith, who for the joy that was set before Him endured the cross, despising the shame, and has sat down at the right hand of the throne of God.

Read that again. We must remember He is the author. Jesus is the finisher. He is Jehovah. The Greek translation for the word finisher is *teleiōtēs*. According to Strong's Concordance finisher is defined as:

1) a perfector
2) one who has in his own person raised faith to its perfection and so set before us the highest example of faith Jesus is the perfector. He has shown us the highest example of

faith. He "has sat down at the right hand of the throne of God". When Jesus said it is finished, in essence He said, "I have set before you my perfect example. I have given my life, in order for you to receive life. I have endured. I was despised, but now I reign as a King. I am your High Priest and Sacrifice. To know me, is to have life that is why I came (Philippians 3:10). Don't let my experience on the cross, become just a sad memory, but instead a solid reality that there is life in me."

So, what is it all for? It is to make sure that when we hear that final trumpet that we will all come fully into life and eternally live in His presence. It is that we receive our final reward-the gift of eternal life. It is essential that we do not have short-term focus; that we begin to shift our focus from living solely for this moment. We must remember that this is a journey in the earth realm that begins in a measurement called time. But there will come a day in which our reality will become our life in eternity. How successful we are will depend strongly on how well we live by faith. God will measure our faith level, works and beliefs. It is our use of faith within the earth that will directly relate to whether we believe God is who He says He is. We cannot merely believe in God, we must have lives that reflect our belief in God. In the good times and in the challenging times, our lives must speak on God's behalf.

One of the most profound statements ever spoken was in a movie called Facing the Giants. During one of the movie scenes the coach is found encouraging the team before a game, and he says, "If we win we will praise Him, and if we lose, we'll still praise Him". Serving God faithfully is found in a consistent life, with eyes focused on Him. Doesn't He deserve it? Think about the nails in His hands. Each nail proved He deserved it What about the crown on His head, does He deserve it? What about the stripes on His back, surely that demonstrates He deserves it. What does He deserve? He deserves our praise and our worship. While we win in life, He deserves praise. When it seems as though we are losing in life, He still deserves our praise. Not only our praise, but also our faithful consistent praise. He is there waiting. Waiting on His throne. Even the Father said, "He seeks a worshipper"-one that will worship Him with their lives.

John 4:23 (NKJV) 23But the hour is coming, and now is, when the true worshipers will worship the Father in spirit and truth; for the Father is seeking such to worship Him.

Our faith in God demonstrates our worship. We have been pulled into the false sense that worship occurs at a special building during a specific time while music is played. Although this is a form of worship, it is not the only form of worship that the Father is seeking. He is looking for those who worship Him because they believe His Word. They worship Him in "spirit and truth". Their lives demonstrate their worship. Whether at work, at home, at church or at school, the one whom the Father seeks; lives a life that testifies that He is who He says He is. If we can remember to remain focused, we will receive a great reward. What an honor to know that we will reign with Him in His Kingdom, an everlasting Kingdom that has no end. A place where there will be no more weeping-a time where all of our tears will be wiped away. A time where we will be given beauty for ashes (Isaiah 61:3). Our faith will help to keep us focused. Our faith will allow us to live here on earth at a level that will give us a glimpse of Heaven. What is it all for? It is to live eternally, with the resurrected Lord and Savior, to finally come home. We are not like Dorothy looking for a yellow brick road, we know the way to the Father. We know that faith in Jesus Christ is the way. Why? Because He said it. Jesus is the way, the truth and life. (John 14:6)

Chapter 13

FAITH IN HIS RESURRECTION

After careful consideration, we can clearly see that faith is important. There is an additional component that is extremely powerful and essential when demonstrating our faith. It is faith in the resurrection of Jesus Christ. Well you are probably wondering why this is so important. Faith in the resurrection is the foundation of our faith. Without the resurrection faith cannot be defined. Without the resurrection Christianity cannot be defined. It is the only unique religion that exists upon a risen Savior. The empty tomb is the foundation of all that we believe in. Without an empty tomb, Christ becomes just another man. Without the empty tomb, we are destined to live an empty life, with death as our conclusion. Without an empty tomb, even creation itself can be doubted. It is fundamental that there is no doubt, that Jesus is the Christ. The stone that covered the tomb was there, but His body was not. Think about this scripture:

Philippians 3:10-11 (NKJV) 10 that I may know Him and the power of His resurrection, and the fellowship of His sufferings, being conformed to His death, 11 if, by any means, I may attain to the resurrection from the dead.

The Apostle Paul makes a profound statement- "that I may know Him and the power of His resurrection". This statement concludes the matter of Christianity and discipleship. The goal of our lives is that we might know Him. The goal of our lives is that we will love and worship Him. But in addition, we must be acquainted with the power of His resurrection. When Jesus Christ rose from the grave He accomplished two goals. He established that God is who He says He is, and He deserves glory and honor. He also established that there is nothing like the power of God. An empty tomb demonstrated the power of God. The Holy Spirit was there demonstrating God's sovereign power. Jesus Christ came as a humble servant, but left the earth as a resurrected powerful King. He demonstrated His power on earth, and in one final moment, He forever put to rest His identity. During His ministry Jesus Christ demonstrated several miracles. Yet, one miracle magnificently spoke to the power of Jesus Christ. Jesus once new a man named Lazarus. Lazarus was the brother of Mary and Martha. Sadly, Lazarus died. What is unusual is not the death of Lazarus, but the circumstances surrounding his death. When Jesus was notified that Lazarus was sick, He shockingly remained where He was an additional two days. One could summarize that Jesus intentionally delayed going to Lazarus. When you take a moment and place yourself in Martha and Mary's shoes, this is not easy to accept. The one person who you know can heal your brother decides to delay His visit. This must have been hard to accept. In verse 4 of John 11 it says,

John 11:4 (NKJV) 4When Jesus heard that, He said, "This sickness is not unto death, but for the glory of God, that the Son of God may be glorified through it."

We can conclude that Jesus knew exactly what would happen. Jesus Christ knew that the goal of Lazarus' death was not death itself, but "that the Son of God may be glorified…" Not only would Lazarus' death glorify Christ, but also His death would demonstrate the Holy Power of the living God. Jesus goes on to say in verse 15 that He is actually glad that He did not arrive in time to heal Lazarus. Jesus knew that although the disciples had seen many miracles, nothing would cause them to believe more than resurrecting a man from the dead. In verse 25 Jesus says to Martha, ***John 11:25-26 (NKJV) 25Jesus said to her, "I am the resurrection and the life. He who believes in Me, though he may die, he shall***

live. 26And whoever lives and believes in Me shall never die. Do you believe this?"

This is a powerful truth spoken by Jesus. He states to us, not only is He King, but He is the resurrection. This scripture is what gives the believer hope. Hope knowing that although we die, and our bodies return to the earth, we will eternally live with Him. This is what it means by knowing the power of His resurrection. It is to know and believe by faith that we will never die. The question is "Do you believe this?"

In verse 27 Martha replies, "Yes, Lord, you are the Christ." Jesus proceeds to do what seems impossible. Have you ever wondered why Jesus wept? Although the scriptures do not literally state why, one thing we can rule out-He did not weep over Lazarus, for He knew that He was going to raise Lazarus from the dead. If Jesus wept because of Lazarus' death, that would suggest that Jesus was not aware of His own power. On the contrary, Jesus knew exactly what was going to take place. In verse 42, Jesus in essence says to the Father, I said these things, not because I doubt you, but I said these things so that the people would believe that I am the Christ. Now take a look back at the scripture, "to know the power of His resurrection". Jesus began with Lazarus, but He ended by demonstrating through His own death that He was and is the Son of God.

Let's think about that for a moment-the power of His resurrection. We must let this reality sink in. Jesus Christ is

Faith In His Resurrection

seated on the throne, on the right hand of the Father, resurrected, alive, and worthy of glory, honor and praise. It is His desire that we might know Him, and that we might believe Him. Remember, He said, "I am the resurrection". He is the way, the truth and the life. Since He has the power to conquer death, we can conclude that He can conquer anything. The question still is, "Do you believe this?" So what is the big deal? Well, it is imperative that we first have faith in the power of His resurrection. If we can believe in His resurrecting power, everything else should be a piece of cake. Think about it. If we believe He could rise again, why is it so hard to believe that He watches over us and cares for our well-being? Believing in His resurrecting power is the foundation of everything else we believe. The easiest way to look at this is to take a look at ourselves. Although not physically dead, hasn't Jesus Christ resurrected you? Isn't His resurrecting power evident in your life? Do you look and act like the same person before He came into your life? Isn't it true that you have a new life in Christ? Just like Lazarus, didn't Jesus call you forth? Yes! Our life goal is that we might know Him and the power of His resurrection. Do you believe this?

So the ultimate question again is, "What is it all for?" Why must we be confident in our belief in God? There is one simple answer to this question. Our level of belief has eternal consequences. Now for those who have not accepted Jesus Christ as their Lord and Savior, the consequences are far more severe. For some, this will mean eternal separation-from God. But those who truly know the risen Savior have a hope that words cannot express. We have the confident assurance, that one-day we will dwell with the Father, Jesus Christ and the Holy Spirit for all eternity. Jesus Christ stated this in the scriptures when He said:

John 14:1-4 (NKJV) 1"Let not your heart be troubled; you believe in God, believe also in Me. 2In My Father's house are many mansions; if it were not so, I would have told you. I go to prepare a place for you. 3And if I go and prepare a place for you, I will come again and receive you to Myself; that where I am, there you may be also. 4And where I go you know, and the way you know."

For those of us who have accepted Jesus Christ in our lives, and have chosen to live by faith, we have an assurance that Jesus Christ has prepared a place for us- in His Father's house. In our Father's house: Jesus Christ will be there-that is the point. That is the reason that we live by faith, in this lifetime. Jesus Christ said, "and the way you know".

The "way" is to live by faith. As challenging as it may seem, our faith and works are the only avenues that we have available, that demonstrate that we believe God. God has placed us here on the earth, but He has stayed connected to us, through His love for us, and our faith and trust in Him. He is faithful to us, watches over us, and cares for us. Through salvation, He has given us the ability and choice to know Him. Everyday, when we choose to live by faith, and not merely by our natural senses, we demonstrate our love and commitment to the Father. We say with our actions, "I love you God, and I believe that you love and care for me". He gives us an opportunity through faith, to rise to higher heights in Him. The point of the matter is that we win!

How do we know that we will win? When you have an opportunity to study the book of Revelations, you will see clearly that we win. Because of our faith in Him, we can look forward to a new city, whose builder and founder is God (Hebrews 11:10). In the book of Revelations, the Apostle John is able to reveal to us all that God has "prepared" for us. Those who finish the race, and live by faith, will dwell with God in a "New Jerusalem". (Revelation 21:10)

Revelation 21:3-4 (NKJV) 3And I heard a loud voice from heaven saying, "Behold, the tabernacle of God is with men, and He will dwell with them, and they shall be His people. God Himself will be with them and be their God. 4And God will wipe away every tear from their eyes; there shall be no more death, nor sorrow, nor crying. There shall be no more pain, for the former things have passed away."

Just imagine- there will be a time where there will be no more pain; a time where sorrow will merely be a memory. A time, just as before, similar to the Garden of Eden, where God will walk among men in the cool of the day. (Genesis 3:8) There will no longer be a need for angels to guard the entrance to the tree of life. (Genesis 3:24) All things will be restored. The original plan of God will manifest. The former things will have passed away. In our new dwelling place, there will not even be a need for a temple. For the Father, Jesus Christ and the Holy Spirit, will be the temple (Revelations 21:22) We must remember that the focus of our love is upon the Father, Jesus Christ, and our heavenly home.

In Revelation 21, John gives us great details, of our new dwelling place with God. John tells us that this new dwelling place will be so glorious, that we will not have need for the Sun or light. Because of God's glory, the Sun is eliminated. Just imagine never having to turn on a light, because darkness will no longer be a reality. Living by faith, will entitle us to become residents of this new city. At last! We will have the opportunity to regain our place in God, which was originally lost in the Garden. The ancient serpent will be destroyed, and all those who were unbelieving will join him in the abyss. So despite our present challenges we can say as Paul said,

2 Corinthians 4:17-18 (NKJV) 17For our light affliction, which is but for a moment, is working for us a far more exceeding and eternal weight of glory, 18while we do not look at the things which are seen, but at the things which are not seen. For the things, which are, seen are temporary, but the things that are not seen are eternal.

At times, what we are going through does not seem like light-afflictions. Sometimes they feel like heavy weights. Sometimes it *feels* as though we cannot make it another day. But we must remember that we have an "eternal weight of glory" to look forward to. No matter the difficulty, no matter the burden, those things are temporary. Our physical challenges, lack of finances, destroyed relationships, stressful jobs are all temporary. We must look forward to a new city, a new dwelling place. But the key portion of the scripture above is verse 18. It is a matter of what we are looking at. We must ask God daily for the ability to change our focus, to clear the lens off of our lives. The problem isn't just our circumstances; it is what we are looking at. Are we looking at the temporary or eternal things? What is the object of our focus?

It is easy for our focus to become blurry in our society. We live in a culture that teaches us, if we can only work hard enough, think long enough, or make just enough, our problems will be solved, and one day we will come to a place of happiness and peace. The real truth is that we will never have true happiness or peace unless we live our lives in continual fellowship with the Father, the Son, and the Holy Spirit. It is God alone, who will give us the rest we are looking for. It is faith in His Son that started it, and it will be faith in His Son that will finish it. There aren't any shortcuts in the life of faith. There are plenty of challenges, plenty of struggles, and plenty of victories. We must remember, that it is like knowing the end of a wonderful love story. Despite the struggles presented in the story, we know that true love wins in the end. It is the same with God. He has written a true love story about us, and it is His true love for us that will cause us to win in the end. The question of the love story is "Do you know your part?" "Do you know your lines?" "Will someone have to be called in to take your role?" God is the author (Hebrews 12:2). He has written a plan guaranteed to make us win; the issue is do you believe it? If you are the just, can you live by faith?

Chapter 14

FAITH...OUR ONLY OPTION

At this point, hopefully, you have taken an evaluation of the level of faith that you are living by. As discussed earlier, when you take a moment and think about it. Is living by faith optional when you are a child of God? Take a moment and think about Abraham. In Genesis God made a covenant with Abraham. At the Father's instruction, Abraham was told to leave his family and country. God instructed him to journey to an unknown land. And in return for his obedience God made six promises to Abraham.

1. God told Abraham that out of his descendants, there would be a great nation
2. God promised to bless Abraham
3. God promised to make Abraham's name great
4. God promised to bless or curse appropriately, friends or enemies of Abraham

5. God promised that from Abraham, all families in him would be blessed

So what is the point? What does this have to do with us? Take a moment and notice the last promise. That is where you and I fit in. God promised that "all families" in Abraham would be blessed. Notice what Paul states in Galatians 3:7,

Galatians 3:7 (NKJV) 7Therefore know that only those who are of faith are sons of Abraham.

To be in the family of Abraham, or adopted as sons (or daughters), we must be of faith. In order to be blessed of God, we must be true descendants of Abraham. Combine the above scripture with this scripture found in verse 14 of the same chapter:

Galatians 3:14 (NKJV) 14that the blessing of Abraham might come upon the Gentiles in Christ Jesus, that we might receive the promise of the Spirit through faith.

To live by faith is the absolute and only way to receive the blessing of Abraham. The "promise of the Spirit" is received only by faith. One thing we know about Abraham is that it was not a confession that was made verbally, but it was by his life, that he demonstrated his faith in Jehovah. The bottom line is, when God said go, Abraham went. When God said, "offer him there as a burnt offering on one of the mountains" (Genesis 22:2); Abraham and Isaac went. The fact that we belong to Christ makes us Abraham's seed. (Galatians 3:29).

Just as we are the seed from our natural fathers, we are the seed of Abraham. We also carry our natural father's DNA, personality traits and characteristics, and we should also carry Abraham's characteristics. We must be "of the faith". As difficult as life may seem at times, we have to "build up our most holy faith" (Jude 1:20). Winds may blow, seasons may change, but building an unwavering faith, is what keeps us in the race. "The race is not given to the swift nor the strong, but to those who endure to the end" (Ecclesiastes 9:11).

To live by faith requires perseverance and endurance. It requires us to tap into a part of our spirit that may be under utilized. Think a minute. If you have children, how difficult is it to decide that you believe God so much that you are willing to sacrifice your child? Well Abraham did. Abraham passed the test, to set an example. This is not a time where God is asking us as believers to sacrifice our children. He already became our perfect sacrifice.

God did what He asked Abraham to do. He did it for me. He did it for you. He sent our Isaac; Jesus Christ the only begotten Son. Jesus Christ, just like Isaac, was willing to lay bound and be offered for us. He did that. God did that-for us. That love, is so amazing. The love that Abraham had for the Father, God turned around and demonstrated to us in the same manner. Now, what does God require of us? The same thing He required from Abraham-that we believe Him, and it be credited unto us for righteousness.

Romans 4:20-25 (NKJV) 20He did not waver at the promise of God through unbelief, but was strengthened in faith, giving glory to God, 21and being fully convinced that what He had promised He was also able to perform. 22And therefore "it was accounted to him for righteousness." 23Now it was not written for his sake alone that it was imputed to him, 24but also for us. It shall be imputed to us who believe in Him who raised up Jesus our Lord from the dead, 25who was delivered up because of our offenses, and was raised because of our justification.

By "not wavering at the promise," we also may be "strengthened in faith," and give "glory to God". Yes, God receives the glory when we live by faith. God receives the glory when we demonstrate, that He is who He says He is. God is given the glory when we are "fully convinced". The beauty is found in verse 23. It says that it was imputed for you- imputed for me. But there is a catch...only if we believe in Him.

There is no doubt, when we look around the world, and when we live in a culture that seems so dark, trying to live by faith, seems almost impossible. Yet, that is what makes it faith. It takes what seems to be impossible and makes it possible. Impossibilities give us a reason to hope. Impossibilities give us a reason to pray. Impossibilities give us a reason to look beyond what is seen to what is unseen. Impossibilities build up our faith. So again, what is the point? Faith is not merely a vehicle that you use to accomplish all of your goals and desires. Faith is a way of life. It began with a confession of your belief in Christ; it will end with a demonstration of your life in Christ. We have to know, beyond a shadow of a doubt, that God is who He says He is.

When we do not know what to do or where to go, we must remember that God is our answer, and by faith we must believe that "He is a rewarder of those who diligently seek Him."

Hebrews 11:6 (NKJV) 6But without faith it is impossible to please Him, for he who comes to God must believe that He is, and that He is a rewarder of those who diligently seek Him.

We must believe that He is. He is what? He is everything we need. Remember what He told Moses when Moses asked, who shall I say sent me? God said, "I AM WHO I AM". In other words we must believe that He is who He says He is. Well the point is, who is God, and what must we believe? Well, Abraham said He was Jehovah Jireh, the Lord who will provide (Genesis 22:14). Hagar said He was Jehovah Roi, the Lord who sees me (Genesis 16:13). King David called-Him, Jehovah Baal Perazim, the Lord who "breaks through my enemies, like the breakthrough of water." (2 Samuel 5:20.) To Joseph, He is El Shaddai, the Almighty God (Genesis 48:3). To Ezekiel, He is Jehovah Shammah, the Lord God who is there (Ezekiel 48:35). To the Prophet Jeremiah,

He is El Olam, the everlasting God (Jeremiah 10:10). To King David He is also Jehovah Raah, the Lord my Shepherd (Psalm 23:1). In the book of Leviticus, it states that He is Jehovah M'Kaddesh, the Lord who sanctifies me (Leviticus 20:8). In the book of Samuel, He is Jehovah Sabaoth, the Lord of Hosts (1 Samuel 1:3). Most of all to Jesus Christ He is "Eloi, Eloi" – He is my God, my God.

So once again what is it all for?

1 Peter 1:18-21 (NKJV) 18knowing that you were not redeemed with corruptible things, like silver or gold, from your aimless conduct received by tradition from your fathers, 19but with the precious blood of Christ, as of a lamb without blemish and without spot. 20He indeed was foreordained before the foundation of the world, but was manifest in these last times for you 21who through Him believe in God, who raised Him from the dead and gave Him glory, so that your faith and hope are in God.

For clarity sake, look at the same scripture in another translation: *1 Peter 1:18-21 (MSNT) 18knowing, as you do, that it was not with a ransom of perishable wealth, such as silver or gold, that you were set free from your frivolous habits of life which had been handed down to you from your forefathers, 19but with the precious blood of Christ—as of an unblemished and spotless lamb. 20He was pre-destined indeed to this work, even before the creation of the world, but has been plainly manifested in these last days for the sake of you who, through Him, 21are faithful to God, who raised Him from among the dead and gave Him glory, so that your faith and hope are resting upon God.*

We live by faith because the precious Lamb of God paid for it. We live by faith because He is Holy and just. We live by faith because we give Him glory. We live by faith, because He is who He says He is. So are you the just? Then live by faith. Are you called? Then live by faith. Are you sons and daughters of the most High God? Then live by faith. Let your life give Him glory, let your life give Him praise-let us all live by faith. Remember this:

Galatians 3:13-14 (MSNT) 13Christ has purchased our freedom from the curse of the Law by becoming accursed for us—because "Cursed is every one who is hanged upon a tree." 14Our freedom has been thus purchased in order that in Christ Jesus the blessing belonging to Abraham may come upon the nations, so that through faith we may receive the promised Spirit.

So what shall we conclude? Through faith, we may receive the promised Spirit, and all that He has for us. Yes, the just must, live by faith…

~

"Your faith
has saved you;
Go in peace."

Luke 7:50

~

CLOUD OF WITNESSES

Hebrews 11:1-40 (KJV) 1Now faith is the substance of things hoped for, the evidence of things not seen. 2For by it the elders obtained a good report. 3Through faith we understand that the worlds were framed by the word of God, so that things which are seen were not made of things which do appear.

4By faith Abel offered unto God a more excellent sacrifice than Cain, by which he obtained witness that he was righteous, God testifying of his gifts: and by it he being dead yet speaketh. 5By faith Enoch was translated that he should not see death; and was not found, because God had translated him: for before his translation he had this testimony, that he pleased God. 6But without faith it is impossible to please him: for he that cometh to God must believe that he is, and that he is a rewarder of them that diligently seek him. 7By faith Noah, being warned of God of things not seen as yet, moved with fear, prepared an ark to the saving of his house; by the which he condemned the world, and became heir of the righteousness which is by faith.

8 By faith Abraham, when he was called to go out into a place which he should after receive for an inheritance, obeyed; and he went out, not knowing whither he went. 9 By faith he sojourned in the land of promise, as in a strange country, dwelling in tabernacles with Isaac and Jacob, the heirs with him of the same promise: 10For he looked for a city which hath foundations, whose builder and maker is God.

11Through faith also Sarah herself received strength to conceive seed, and was delivered of a child when she was past age, because she judged him faithful who had promised. 12Therefore sprang there even of one, and him as good as dead, so many as the stars of the sky in multitude, and as the sand which is by the sea shore innumerable. 13These all died in faith, not having received the promises, but having seen them afar off, and were persuaded of them, and embraced them, and confessed that they were strangers and pilgrims on the earth. 14For they that say such things declare plainly that they seek a country. 15And truly, if they had been mindful of that country from whence they came out, they might have had opportunity to have returned. 16But now they desire a better country, that is, an heavenly: wherefore God is not ashamed to be called their God: for he hath prepared for them a city.

17By faith Abraham, when he was tried, offered up Isaac: and he that had received the promises offered up his only begotten son, 18Of whom it was said, That in Isaac shall thy seed be called: 19Accounting that God was able to raise him up, even from the dead; from whence also he received him in a figure. 20By faith Isaac blessed Jacob and Esau concerning things to come. 21By faith Jacob, when he was a dying, blessed both the sons of Joseph; and worshipped, leaning upon the top of his staff. 22By faith Joseph, when he died, made mention of the departing of the children of Israel; and gave commandment concerning his bones.

23By faith Moses, when he was born, was hid three months of his parents, because they saw he was a proper child; and they were not afraid of the king's commandment. 24By faith Moses, when he was come to years, refused to be called the son of Pharaoh's daughter; 25Choosing rather to suffer affliction with the people of God, than to enjoy the pleasures of sin for a season; 26Esteeming the reproach of Christ greater riches than the treasures in Egypt: for he had respect unto the recompense of the reward. 27By faith he forsook Egypt, not fearing the wrath of the king: for he endured, as seeing him who is invisible. 28Through faith he kept the passover, and the sprinkling of blood, lest he that destroyed the firstborn should touch them. 29By faith they passed through the Red sea as by dry land: which the Egyptians assaying to do were drowned. 30By faith the walls of Jericho fell down, after they were compassed about seven days.

31By faith the harlot Rahab perished not with them that believed not, when she had received the spies with peace. 32And what shall I more say? for the time would fail me to tell of Gideon, and of Barak, and of Samson, and of Jephthae; of David also, and Samuel, and of the prophets: 33Who through faith subdued kingdoms, wrought righteousness, obtained promises, stopped the mouths of lions, 34Quenched the violence of fire, escaped the edge of the sword, out of weakness were made strong, waxed valiant in fight, turned to flight the armies of the aliens. 35Women received their dead raised to life again: and others were tortured, not accepting deliverance; that they might obtain a better resurrection: 36And others had trial of cruel mockings and scourgings, yea, moreover of bonds and imprisonment: 37They were stoned, they were sawn asunder, were tempted, were slain with the sword: they wandered about in sheepskins and goatskins; being destitute, afflicted, tormented; 38(Of whom the world was not worthy:) they wandered in deserts, and in mountains, and in dens and caves of the earth. 39And these all, having obtained a good report through faith, received not the promise: 40God having provided some better thing for us, that they without us should not be made perfect.

CONFESSION OF FAITH
Power of the spoken word

"I will declare the decree of the Lord" – Psalm 2

I am known by my Father, because He knew me before I was born, and before the foundations were laid. (Jer 1:5)

I am reconciled to the Father, by the blood of the Lamb: Jesus Christ. (Colossians 1:20)

I have the Holy Spirit, and the Lord's Spirit is working in me to renew my thoughts, and create my life through Christ Jesus. (John 10:10, Romans 12:2)

I will daily seek the presence of God. His presence is my shield. Through His presence I am positioned for my day, and apart from Him I can do nothing. (John 15:5)

I am God's Holy tabernacle, and I daily carry His presence. (Deuteronomy 33:29, John 15:5, I Corinthians 6:19)

God has given me 1,440 minutes in a day. I seek to be a good steward over my time, and declare that satan, nor the world will distract me from that which God has for me. (John 9:4)

I am a joint-heir with Christ, and all that belongs to Him be- longs to me. (Romans 8:16-17)

My destination is Heaven, while the earth is my journey, I press forward to the mark of my high calling. (Philippians 3:14)

I was raised with Christ, and I am seated in the heavenlies, for He raised me through the power of His resurrection. (Galatians 2:20)

Jesus Christ and the Father have made their home with me because I love them and keep His Word. (John 14:23)

The Holy Spirit lives in me, and He is my Counselor, teacher, and Spirit of truth. (John 14)

I live by faith, because I was justified by Christ, and the just shall live by faith. (Habakkuk 2:4)

My body is the temple of God-nothing unholy or harmful shall approach me. (I Corinthians 3:16)

I have the fruit of self-control. Nothing external shall dominate me. The lust of the eye, the lust of the flesh, the pride of life, will not infiltrate my life. (2 Peter 1:6)

Excessiveness will not dominate me. Neither food nor anything material shall dominate me. I have the power from the

Confession of Faith

Father to live a life of freedom. I keep my body under subjection, through the power of God. (I Corinthians 9:27)

I walk in the Spirit. My flesh shall not dominate. As in the spirit of Esau and Jacob; the elder shall serve the younger. My flesh shall serve my spirit. (Galatians 5:16, Genesis 25:23)

The Lord gave me a healthy mind. I believe that God will help me to manage my thought life. (Philippians 2:5)

I was crucified with Christ, now I live my life through the Spirit, and for His glory. (Galatians 2:20)

My God is a consuming fire. He baptizes me with fire, so that He may purify me like gold. He seeks to cut away those things that hinder me from producing His fruit. I yield to this baptism of fire. (Hebrews 12:29)

I seek first the Kingdom of God, His ways, His thinking, His characteristics, and all things needed and desired will be added unto me. (Matthew 6:33)

I seek to reproduce the faithful love God has for me, for others. I seek to demonstrate, the power of God's love in my life. (Psalm 103)

I trust in the Lord with all my heart. Doubt and my own understanding I refuse to live by and base decisions on. I seek

Him with my heart, and He tells me the way I should go. (Proverbs 3:5-6)

I allow God to fill my mouth with His words; I speak forth whatever He tells me. (Jeremiah 1, Ezekiel 37:9)

I have the power, given by the Holy Trinity, to abolish and destroy every demonic force that comes against my family or myself. (Luke 10:19)

Today I bind every demonic force that seeks to hinder my-self, family, extended family, or Kingdom family, and I loose the power of Jesus Christ in our lives. Since my God protects me, when satan seeks to destroy me, he will be defeated by the power of Jesus Christ and fall. (Matthew 18:18, John 18:6)

I ask the Lord to rebuke satan from my life and from the lives of my family and the family of God this day. (Jude1:9)

I seek to obey the Father, and give my life, as He has given His. (I Samuel 5:22)

I shall not live by fear, because fear is the enemy of my faith. (II Timothy 1:7)

I shall not be moved by what I see. I will remain immovable, planted like a tree, abounding toward good works, and prospering in all that I do. (Psalm 1)

Confession of Faith

I think about the Lord and His instruction, during the morning, in the afternoon, and in the evening, therefore all that I do will prosper. (Psalm 1)

I study God's Word, and I look intently. I don't forget, and I am a doer, therefore I will be blessed in whatever I do. (James 1:25)

The peace of God, shall cover me like a shield. I will dwell in that place, like the land of Goshen, where prosperity, and goodness will abound. (Genesis 47:27)

I have everything I need, that pertains to this life. I do not rule from my position on earth, but I reign with Christ from a heavenly position. (2 Peter 1:3)

The Lord will prosper the work of my (our hands), He blesses it, so that we have a supernatural supply that will never run out. The 12 basketful leftover concept is evident in our lives. We tap into a heavenly supply, which exceeds our earthly possessions. (Luke 9:17)

We access our spiritual blessings by faith. Everything we need is supplied according to His riches in Heaven, and will manifest in our lives. (2 Corinthians 5:7)

The Lord's favor leads me and follows me. Favor makes a way, when there is no way. Favor helps me to cross over on dry ground into the Lord's destination. (Lk 1:28, Ex 15:19)

The Lord is my rear guard, He sits on the throne, an watches over me. He intercedes on my behalf, and is my strength when I am weak. (Exodus 14:19, 2 Corinthians 12:9, Hebrews 4:14)

My family is the inheritance of the Lord. We represent His Kingdom. We are citizens of His Kingdom, and our lifestyles testify to the goodness of the Lord. (Psalm 127:3)

My children are blessed of the Lord. The garment of praise and holiness shall be theirs. They are obedient to His Word, and seek to do His will. A stranger's voice, they will not follow. They are like sheep among wolves, but the Lord is their defender-a very present help in a time of trouble. They will look to Him, when they don't know what to do, and He shall lead them, as a shepherd leading his flock. They are the Lord's inheritance. (Isaiah 61:3, John 10:5, Psalm 46:1)

I will seek to instruct my children in the way they should go. They will know, that Jesus is the way, the truth and the life. He will prepare a place for them. (Genesis 18:19)

I will praise and worship the Lord. Not merely with a song, but with my life. My life, will demonstrate His praise, and His worship. Our lives will show others, that God is worthy of our worship and praise. (Psalm 29:2)

Like God stated in the beginning, I know that I am created

in His image and likeness. So in the same manner that He spoke over creation, I speak over my life and say,

Let there be peace,
Let there be prosperity, Let there be excellent health, Let there be love,
Let there be joy,
Let there be faith, and hope, in my family and the family of God

And like the Lord, I looked, and saw all that my words created, and saw that "It was good." (Genesis 1)

Every word I have spoken is decreed, it is declared, it is sealed, and therefore established. (Job 22:28)

Now, in the name of Jesus Christ, and in the power of the Holy Spirit, I seal this confession, Amen.

www.ingramcontent.com/pod-product-compliance
Lightning Source LLC
Chambersburg PA
CBHW061656040426
42446CB00010B/1759